Practically Human

Practically Human

College Professors Speak from the Heart of Humanities Education

Gary Schmidt and Matthew Walhout
Editors

the CALVIN
COLLEGE PRESS

Grand Rapids, Michigan • calvincollegepress.com

Published 2012 by the Calvin College Press
PO Box 888200
Kentwood, MI 49588

Printed in the United States of America

Publisher's Cataloging-in-Publication Data
Practically human : college professors speak from the heart of humanities education / edited by Gary Schmidt and Matthew Walhout.

  p.   cm.
  ISBN 9781937555030 (pbk.)
1. Education, Humanistic—United States. 2. Classical education—United States. 3. Humanities—Study and teaching—United States. 4. Church and college—United States. I. Schmidt, Gary. II. Walhout, Matthew. III. Title.

LC1011 .P73 2012
370.11/2—dc23

Library of Congress Control Number: 2012937061

Cover design: Robert Alderink
Cover image: Erland Sibuea, *Complexity*, 2009, acrylic on canvas, 19¾ × 19¾ in. Private Collection. Used by permission.

For

Clarence Walhout,

father to one of the editors,

colleague to the other,

model to both,

who has shown what it means to be

a humane teacher and scholar.

CONTENTS

About This Book

If you are a student wondering what to study in college, this book is for you. It invites you to seek out the practical benefits of studying literature, language, the arts, history, religion, and philosophy. These disciplines—known collectively as the humanities—will teach you to analyze complex social dynamics, articulate good arguments, and apply the hard-won wisdom of the past to new and challenging situations.

Learning of this kind will produce a deep and versatile intelligence that will serve you well in whatever profession you choose. Just as importantly, this same, discerning intelligence will help you evaluate what your culture offers, make good decisions, and maintain healthy relationships. And as a bonus, you may find that you love reading literature, contemplating the arts, and learning about other cultures, times, and places. This book gives you specific examples of how these personal, interpersonal, and professional benefits can emerge within particular subject areas of the humanities.

It should be said up front that the authors of the essays in this collection share a Christian understanding of human nature and human flourishing. All of them are professors at a Christian college, and their common faith commitment fuels their love of teaching and writing. They have found their callings, their vocations, in such work, and they want to help students sort through a variety of vocational possibilities.

If you are not a student yourself but want to give guidance to one, this book is also for you. Parents may wish to read it in order to understand a student's tastes and to see how the humanities connect with career choices. Student groups in schools or churches might use it as a way of clarifying and reflecting upon the hopes and expectations that they bring to college. If you are a guidance counselor, or if you work in youth ministries, you may want to use the book as a resource in advising and mentoring. Or if you are a high school teacher, you might have students read and discuss the chapters that relate to your discipline. A group of humanities teachers might even use the book as common touchstone for various courses. Such an approach could be an effective way of unifying the "Christian perspectives" curriculum of a Christian high school.

The authors hope anyone who reads this book will get a glimpse of some of the rich learning experiences that college can offer. They also hope to show how the stories and wisdom of human communities are shared, enriched, and renewed through the learning process.

Additional Resources

For additional materials, including information about the authors, see http://www.calvincollegepress.com/practically human.

Introduction

Two Farms

One of the oldest houses in western Michigan is a farmhouse built during the early 1830s on a plot of land that the locals still call the Buck Farm, after its first owner. The house has sprouted several additions over the years, starting with a second story that was constructed around the time of the Civil War. Throughout the history of its renovations, this house has had a single purpose: it was designed to be a family home. Today, if Mr. Buck could peek in through the kitchen window in the early evening, he would be likely to find a mother, a father, and their children sitting around a dinner table, precisely where he and his family sat nearly two centuries ago.

Thanks mainly to the sandy soil, agriculture has never been the Buck Farm's strong suit. Mr. Buck was a stagecoach driver and grew barely enough hay to feed his horses. The mother and father who live there now make a living by teaching and writing; the farm does give them sustenance, but mostly in the form of peaceful respite, creative inspiration, and a wholesome country atmosphere. Conventional wisdom would say that the Buck Farm has always been impractical, that it has failed in the farming business. But does a farm have to be a business? Does its profit have to be measured in cash flow? Or is there more to be cultivated on a farm than crops and cattle?

Most weekdays, the father who lives at the Buck Farm drives to the campus of Calvin College, where he teaches English literature and composition, and which happens to be located on the site of another former farm, the Knollcrest Farm. Like the English teacher, this college roots itself in a particular understanding of what it means to live a fulfilling and meaningful life. Like him, it has dedicated its land to the growth and flourishing of human beings. And its use of land, too, gets drawn into question by conventional measures of productivity.

Colleges like Calvin face a constant barrage of questions and criticisms in the mass media, all suggesting that higher education wastes resources. The criticism focuses on the supposedly "impractical" fields known as the humanities: history, philosophy, cultural studies, languages, and, yes, the English teacher's own areas of literature and composition. What jobs can a student get after graduating with a degree in art history? What marketable skills can one develop by reading ancient books like Plato's *Republic*? Why take a composition class in college if you want to pursue a career that doesn't require much writing? It seems like the humanities don't enhance anyone's earning potential very much; so why bother with these subjects at all?

The English teacher and his colleagues have their own answers to these questions, a few of which are on display in the pages of this book. These teachers went into their fields for good reason, most importantly because they enjoy learning, studying, and helping students understand the great ideas that enliven the cultural world of human societies. Think of it this way: these great ideas are like the soil in which human beings grow. A humanities education is like fertilizer that strengthens a student's intellectual roots, increases resistance to disease, and enhances the production of good fruit.

The cultivation metaphor resonates with the teachers at Calvin College, because they share a single great idea about human purpose—a religious conception of what all people, including students, are for. The idea is that people are created to glorify the God who created and redeemed them, and to share the love of this God with others in the world. The humanities are meant to serve these purposes, to help people become who they are supposed to be, to help them grow as human beings.

So the main concern at the former Buck and Knollcrest Farms is not about cash crops but rather about what Christians call fruits of the Spirit. These fruits are the bounty that the teachers hope for, and this book is a testament to that bounty.

In the essays presented here, several professors from Calvin College provide glimpses into their classrooms and their areas of study, and they share stories about students being challenged, strengthened, and blessed by academic learning experiences. Each chapter invites the reader to reassess and reaffirm the value of the humanities. The essays are for anyone who is thinking about how to choose a college, or whether to major in a certain subject, or just which humanities courses to take. They are for parents, teachers, and guidance counselors, as well as for students.

Practical concerns are not forgotten in any of this. Mr. Buck didn't drive a stagecoach just because he loved horses and carriage rides. He needed to make money. That same need is on the mind of every young adult these days, and a college education is widely seen as a preferred way of gaining employable skills. Unless you are independently wealthy or have decided to follow Thoreau to your own Walden Pond, it is likely that you enter college hoping to find job prospects greeting you on the other side. Few people can escape the need for gainful employment. For many, if not most, this practical concern is a dominant factor in the major decisions of adult life.

Fortunately, students do not have to choose between developing job skills and developing character. This is not an either-or proposition. A college is not a factory farm that cranks out intellectually fattened graduates to be consumed in the labor market. Neither is it a glorified extension of summer camp, where young adults can escape rigorous discipline or prolong their childhood. Instead, a college education should weave together two very serious, very real goals. It should prepare you for a career, and it should also give you wisdom for the life you will live both within and beyond the workplace.

There are places where this kind of preparation can happen. Think of the Buck Farm, where a stagecoach driver raised both his horses and his family, and where a mother and father now find the inspiration and peace of mind that allow them to practice their craft of writing. The old Knollcrest Farm is a similar sort of place, and Calvin College is the home that has been built there. It is home to nearly 4,000 students and 300 teachers who share a unified Christian vision of what it means to be human, a vision that motivates them to seek a healthy balance in their pursuits. Just as a family needs an income, a dinner table, a schedule of chores, and time for recreation, this learning community needs a well-balanced combination of technical focus, joyful fascination, and lofty reflection on the purpose of it all. In the competitive, sometimes inhumane world of higher education, this kind of balance is a basic human need and thus a very practical concern. Calvin and other Christian colleges are in the business of trying to get it right.

For many years the tallest structure on the Calvin campus was the Science Building, which is located at one edge of a well-manicured central green space known as the Commons Lawn. In the basement of that building there is a room whose concrete walls and floor are supported by direct contact with the surrounding hard-packed dirt. This connection to the building's foundation makes the room ideal for physics experiments that might otherwise be hampered by vibrations. Such work cannot be done on the shaky upper floors, where the commotion of footsteps, slamming doors, and moving elevators produces a cacophony of structural noise. But in that basement laboratory there is no problem, because the subterranean earth provides stability and eliminates vibration.

These days the room is home to a team of experimenters—a physics teacher and a handful of students—who are exploring how to use lasers to build a new and very delicate kind of molecule. Besides contributing to significant scientific discoveries, the students are gaining practical knowledge that will help them in their careers. But as they work, their discussions turn frequently to the connections they see between science and other subjects, like history, literature, and philosophy. The connections fascinate them and seem to make science all the more meaningful and worthwhile. For his part, the physics professor welcomes the added value that seeps into the lab from the humanities curriculum. So he encourages these conversations, counting them as an extra measure of educational success. That is the way his lab works, nestled as it is in the soils of the old Knollcrest Farm, which press in on it and hold it steady.

Some time ago a new college chapel was constructed just across the Commons Lawn from the Science Building and became a contender for the title of "tallest building on campus." By all accounts, this was only fitting. While the sciences play a prominent role in the college's educational project, they wear no curricular crown. They are an important part of the overall balance, but they do not dictate it. The campus architecture now reflects this thinking, as all buildings are grounded in the same earth and overshadowed by the same chapel spire.

The physics teacher and the English teacher are dedicated to the mission of their college for one and the same reason: upon this plot of rededicated farmland, they have both found a place to call home. It is a place where both of them can flourish as professionals and as people, a place where they find inspiration and peace of mind, a place where they are supported and stabilized.

Most importantly, this college is a gathering place for people who share a deep commitment to each other and to the God they serve. One of the key goals of the community is to articulate and enliven that commitment and to pass it down from one generation to the next. The essays appearing in this book are part of that project. The authors tell about their experiences and subject areas in the hope that their passions will be contagious. For they can still remember what it was like to wonder about the future. And they can still recall how their own teachers inspired them to make the most of their college years.

If, somehow, that past generation of teachers could hover over the old Knollcrest Farm, as if to form one great cloud of witnesses, what a sight they would see. Like the transfigured Mr. Buck peering into the kitchen of his old farmhouse, they would find a group of people gathered together around a common purpose, giving thanks for their sustenance, and taking in the nourishment they need in order to become more thoughtfully and more practically human.

This is an image of what a college education can offer.

We invite you to partake.

Gary Schmidt, English teacher
Matthew Walhout, physics teacher

Grand Rapids, Michigan
Advent 2011

Greater Than Gold
The Humanities and the Human Things

Lee Hardy, Philosophy

A s a college student in Chicago, I had a summer job delivering flowers for a flower wholesaler. Every weekday I reported to work around six in the morning, loaded up the day's order of flowers in boxes layered with crushed ice, and took off in my step van for the south side, visiting flower shops from 127th Street up to the Loop. My last stop was often the flower shop in the subway station at State and Randolph. I would pull up my van curbside, put on the flashers, and descend into the crowded Chicago subway system with a box on my shoulder about the size of a child's casket. Coming back, I would take the Randolph on-ramp to the Kennedy Expressway heading south. The Kennedy ran below street level at that point, and the on-ramp merged from the left—fast-lane traffic to my right, a high and unforgiving concrete wall to my left. I had about 50 yards to merge. I also had a van with no rear windows and a right side-view mirror with no glass. Repairs were not high on my employer's priority list. So I would make my descent blind, reach what I thought was the general speed of the surrounding traffic, ease right, and listen for horns.

One summer morning I was starting my route, taking Highway 57 north till it merged with the Dan Ryan Expressway. This was another merge-from-the-left scenario. But coming into the Dan Ryan at this juncture I had my own lane and plenty of time to work my way to the right. Which I did—and was promptly lit up by a Chicago cop, who signaled me to pull over. He eased ahead of me on the shoulder of the highway and stopped, but didn't get out of his cruiser. He waved me into the passenger seat. "You were traveling in the left lane about a half-mile back," he said.

"I know," I replied, "I was coming in from 57, so I had to be in the left lane for while."

"Well, that's illegal for a truck, traveling in the left lane."

"Oh," I said, wondering where this conversation was going.

"Are you bonded?" he asked.

"I guess I am." I had no idea if I was bonded or not, or what exactly that meant.

"I could take you down to the station right now, you know," said the cop, his voice taking on a menacing tone.

"I guess you could," I said, being by nature an agreeable sort. The exchange went on like this for about ten minutes. Then, with an air of disgust, he told me to get out. I walked back to my van in a state of confusion. Why didn't he just give me a ticket and be done with it?

Years later, as a rookie philosophy instructor at Calvin College, I was informed in the middle of the fall semester that I had to submit a course proposal for the January Interim, and that the proposal was due in two days. Without much time to think it over, I decided to do a course on the topic of work and vocation. Interim is a kind of curricular free-for-all at Calvin; professors can teach outside of their areas of specialization, and students can take courses outside their majors or programs on a pass/fail basis, just out of interest. To this day it remains a valuable part of a

Calvin undergraduate education. Work, and the meaning of work, was of interest to me. My father owned his own business, and work in that business was the dominant reality of my childhood. I handed in my course description and put in my book order, which included a popular book at the time: *Working*, by Chicago journalist Studs Terkel. It was a collection of fascinating interviews with working people in the Chicago area about their jobs, from bathroom attendants to fashion models.

One interview was conducted with a Chicago truck driver. I read it with special interest. About halfway through the piece the trucker mentioned the interchange of Highway 57 and the Dan Ryan. Yes, I knew that stretch of road well. I read on. He said that Chicago cops would often lie in wait for truckers at that intersection because truckers had to travel illegally in the left lane of the Dan Ryan for at least a couple hundred yards. The cops routinely pulled them over and solicited bribes.

Reading that sentence was like finding a light switch for a small dark room in the back of my growing house of memories. It made complete sense of my strange experience on that summer morning on the Dan Ryan, an experience that had mystified me for years. Having grown up in the 1950s and '60s watching *Leave it to Beaver* and *The Andy Griffith Show*, I thought that cops were honest enforcers of the law, completely trustworthy guys, upright citizens who help elementary school children cross streets and return lost dogs to their distraught owners. The idea that cops would cross the line, that they would solicit people for bribes—that they could be criminals—was completely incomprehensible to me.

I related the experience to my students in the January Interim course. It goes to show you, I said, how literature can illuminate life. And sometimes make it more complex, I thought to myself. Maybe the world isn't divided so neatly into good guys and bad guys, white hats and black hats, saints and sinners; maybe the line between good and evil, as the Russian author Alexander Solzhenitsyn claimed, runs through every human heart.

The Art of Questioning

Sometimes the written word illuminates life by providing answers to questions we bring with us. But sometimes, and often more importantly, what we read can raise questions we've never asked ourselves before—questions that stretch us and change us; questions that significantly alter our sense of self and the world we live in; questions we've never thought of before; questions we vaguely sensed but didn't know how to put into words; perhaps questions that occurred to us but we didn't want to pursue because they'd make life difficult.

My discipline, that part of the humanities known as philosophy, specializes in the art of questioning. Not that philosophers don't propose answers. They do. They propose lots of answers, lots of different answers. But often those answers are responses to questions philosophers have been asking for a long time. In fact, the founder of the discipline of philosophy as we know it in the West, Socrates, devoted his life to asking questions, difficult questions, of others. He didn't write books. He didn't give lectures. He didn't consider himself wise enough to do that. For the most part, he just asked questions of his fellow citizens in ancient Athens, hoping to learn from them, or learn with them, the nature of such things as love, justice, happiness, friendship, and piety. And that's what got him into trouble with the authorities. Eventually, in his old age, he was put on trial. He was found guilty of the charges brought against him. And he was executed.

We might think that the charges against Socrates must have been pretty serious if they were to warrant the death sentence. But it's unlikely they would strike us as capital crimes. Socrates was charged with corrupting the minds of the youth and with impiety. And, as it turns out, both of these charges were based on his passion for asking questions. He wasn't posting obscene images to minors, nor was he spraying graffiti on the walls of Greek temples. He was simply asking pointed questions about the dominant values of his culture (this counted as corrupting the minds of the youth); he openly wondered about the truth of the often scandalous tales the poets and storytellers told of the Greek gods (this counted as impiety). He was, in short, put to death for doing philosophy.

To be fair, the severity of the sentence was due in part to the way the local justice system worked back then (and the surprising move Socrates made within that system). A citizen of Athens was tried by a jury of 501 peers. The jury decided not only on the guilt of the defendant but also on the sentence if the defendant was found guilty. In the interest of coming up with an appropriate sentence, the Athenian court would ask both the prosecutor and the defendant to propose a punishment. The idea was that the prosecutor would propose a sentence that was harsh, but not too harsh, and that the defendant would propose a sentence that was lenient, but not too lenient. Both would tend toward moderation, and the jury would choose between the two.

But things didn't go that way in this case. Having won the conviction, the prosecutor smelled blood and overplayed his hand. He proposed the death sentence. Now it was Socrates's turn to propose a more reasonable penalty. But he didn't. In light of the serious nature of my crimes, Socrates said, I think the city of Athens should provide me every day with a free lunch downtown. Obviously, Socrates was using the sentencing phase of the trial to make his point: his habit of philosophical questioning, as he understood it, was a public service; he had been assigned by the gods to serve as a gadfly to pester the complacent horse of Athens, to keep it on its toes, or, in this case, on its hoofs. So, if he had been found guilty of doing philosophy, it was only fitting that he should receive public support. Clearly the jury couldn't go for Socrates's proposed punishment—it was no punishment at all.

Still, we might ask, why the death sentence? Why were some people so anxious to get rid of Socrates? He was just an old man, after all, standing around in the marketplace of Athens, asking questions. What's the harm in that? Socrates gave his own answer to these questions in his defense before the jury of his peers, a defense that was recorded and lifted to the level of art by his devoted student, Plato. There Socrates reports that a friend of his had gone to the oracle at Delphi and asked if there was anyone wiser than Socrates in the land. The oracle replied that there was indeed no one wiser than Socrates. The oracle at the temple of Delphi was often consulted by people with pressing questions. They would pose the question, and the priestess would return with the answer given by the god. Often, however, the answers were ambiguous and hard to understand. Once a Greek general, whose army was poised for battle, went to the oracle to ask if he should attack the next day. The oracle answered, "If you attack, a great victory will be won." Greatly encouraged, the general returned to the field and attacked the next day. And a great victory was indeed won—by the other side.

Unlike the general, who apparently had no ear for ambiguity, Socrates was genuinely perplexed by the answer given by the god. How can this answer be true, Socrates wondered, for I am only too aware of my own ignorance. So he set out to prove the god wrong by asking pointed questions about the basic values of his fellow citizens. He focused his efforts on the politicians of the day, who seemed especially self-assured in their knowledge of right and wrong, of good and evil, of justice and injustice. Upon public questioning, however, the politicians made it abundantly clear to all in earshot that they didn't know what they were talking about. Although they were quick to condemn actions they disagreed with as unjust, and to promote proposals they favored in the name of justice, they hadn't really thought about the nature of justice and injustice, nor could they give a satisfying account of the nature of either. They had their opinions, to be sure, but no knowledge.

By humiliating public figures in this way, Socrates made a lot of enemies. But this exercise also made clear to him what the oracle meant. He was the wisest of all at least in this small regard: it is unlikely that he or those he engaged in conversation knew anything of much value, but while others thought they knew what they didn't know, he didn't think he knew what he didn't know. This kind of wisdom he called "human wisdom," as opposed to divine wisdom. And that kind of wisdom stands at the beginning of the discipline of philosophy, understood as the search for knowledge. For why would we bother searching for knowledge if we thought we already had it? Growth in genuine knowledge presupposes a good measure of humility. We begin by admitting there is much we do not understand.

A case in point can be found in another artful record of a conversation Socrates had with a local priest by the name of Euthyphro. The conversation took place in front of the municipal courthouse, just before Socrates was to go to trial. He had been charged with impiety, among other things. Surely a priest like Euthyphro would know what piety and impiety are, and that knowledge would surely come in handy as Socrates prepared his defense. It will probably come as no surprise that Socrates was disappointed in his efforts to receive instruction from the priest on the nature of piety.

What Socrates wanted to know was the nature or the form of piety. By the "form of piety" he meant the characteristic, quality, or property that makes a person or an action pious, in short, the "pious-making" property. Once Euthyphro understood what Socrates was asking for, he ventured this definition: the pious is what is loved by the gods. This is to say that being-loved-by-the-gods is the pious-making property. If I perform an action, and it is loved by the gods, then its being-loved-by-the-gods makes it pious. Socrates wonders: Does this definition sit well with the other things Euthyphro believes about the gods? Following the poets, Euthyphro would believe that the gods are often at war with each other, often in conflict. And this divine conflict wouldn't happen unless the gods disagreed on what is to be loved and what is to be hated. So, on Euthyphro's definition of piety, one and the same action could be both pious (because it is loved by some of the gods) and impious (because it is hated by other gods). But this would seem to be a manifest contradiction: one and the same action cannot be both pious and impious.

Euthyphro goes back to the drawing board. He modifies his definition to avoid the contradiction. Now he will claim that the pious is what is loved by *all* the gods. But Socrates wonders again: Is being loved by all the gods really what *makes* an action pious? Perhaps it is true that pious actions are loved by all the gods, but is that what *makes* them pious? Wouldn't it be more appropriate to say that an action is loved by all the gods because it is pious, rather than it is pious because it is loved by all the gods? Euthyphro concedes the point. He then ventures another definition that, upon examination, turns out to be no different than the definition that just went down in flames. At this point in the dialogue Socrates becomes convinced that Euthyphro is toying with him: Surely Euthyphro must know what piety is. He is a priest after all, in the piety business. So, Euthyphro, let's stop playing games. Just tell me what piety is so I can defend myself in court against the charges of impiety. Upon hearing this request, Euthyphro announces that he has to go attend to some other business. And Socrates is left in the lurch.

After reading this dialogue, we might wonder why Plato bothered writing it. Several definitions of piety are tried and found wanting, and then it ends. No one finds out what piety is. What's the point of that? Neither Socrates nor Plato seems to have anything to say about the topic under discussion. But maybe that's just the point. Recall the peculiar kind of human wisdom Socrates possessed: not to think that you know something when you don't. Many of the dialogue's readers probably agreed with Euthyphro in his opinions on the nature of the pious. Then they witnessed those opinions fall apart under examination. By the end of the dialogue they may have realized that they really didn't know what piety is, although they thought they did. But in this very realization lies the invitation to philosophy, to the quest for knowledge, to the search for wisdom.

The Most Important Things

In the Old Testament book of Proverbs, we find a similar emphasis on the importance of wisdom and the value of searching for it: "For wisdom is better than jewels, and all that you may desire cannot compare with her" (Proverbs 8:11); "How much better to get wisdom than gold!" (Proverbs 16:16). Most of us can understand the value of gold—we get an education to get a good job to make good money. But why rank wisdom so highly? Why rank it above money? You can get anything you want, it seems, with enough money. What can you get with wisdom?

Try thinking of it this way: You could have all the goods of this world, but if you were foolish, they would do you no good. There are many who are rich (and famous and powerful) who are also perfectly miserable creatures, who live outstandingly terrible lives. On the other hand, even if you were blessed with very few goods of this world, if you had wisdom, you could still have a good life, for by wisdom you will discern your way in life with understanding (Proverbs 14:8); if you find wisdom, "there will be a future, and your hope will not be cut off" (Proverbs 24:14).

In his defense at trial, Socrates addressed his fellow citizens after he was sentenced to death. Nothing, he said, not even the threat of death, would deter him from doing philosophy, from exhorting those he would meet on the streets: "Good Sir, you are an Athenian, a citizen of the greatest city with the greatest reputation for both wisdom and power; are you not ashamed of your eagerness to possess as much wealth, reputation and honors as possible, while you do not care for nor give thought to wisdom or truth, or the best possible state of your soul?" (Plato's *Apology* 29 d–e). The fact that so many of his fellow citizens pass by wisdom in their rush for wealth, power and fame was a sign to Socrates of the wrong priorities: attaching "little importance to the most important things and greater importance to inferior things" (*Apology* 30 a).

The humanities are among the places where "the most important things" are pondered. History, philosophy, literature, theology, and the arts: these are the academic sites where basic human questions are posed, and where the traditions of wisdom that have developed in response to these questions are explored. Among those wisdom traditions stands the Christian tradition, guided by the Word of God, nourished by generations of reflection on the nature of love, justice, freedom, friendship, happiness, truth, and virtue. This tradition is embedded in texts, rituals, and works of art, waiting to bestow its benefits on all who recognize its value and take the time to dip into its considerable resources. For there too, in the college humanities curriculum, wisdom cries out, as it did in the streets and marketplaces of old: "If you receive my words and treasure up my commandments with you, making your ear attentive to wisdom and inclining your heart to understanding; then you will understand righteousness and justice and equity, every good path; for wisdom will come into your heart, and knowledge will be pleasant to your soul" (Proverbs 2:1, 2; 9, 10).

Granted, we need gold in order to live. Granted, we need a job to haul in the gold. Granted, we need a professional education to get a good job. But to live a good life we need wisdom even more. In college we can learn how to be smart and successful professionals; but at a college with strong offerings in the humanities, we can also learn how to be wise and thoughtful human beings. And that's an education not just for work, but for life.

"The Ducks Are Hazards in the Classroom"
Learning to Listen with Perception and Grace

Benita Wolters-Fredlund, Music

Have you ever laughed hysterically over a misunderstood music lyric? If not—or if so—check out www.kissthisguy.com for a few chuckles. It's an archive of misheard lyrics, named after the most commonly misheard lyric of all time, "Excuse me while I kiss this guy," from Jimi Hendrix's "Purple Haze." (Hendrix actually sings "Excuse me while I kiss the sky.") Rock stars don't generally value enunciation, and they often write poetic, nonliteral texts that are hard to decipher. The result is that even famous pop music icons are routinely understood to be saying silly things they never intended, like

"The ants are my friends, they're blowin' in the wind . . ."
Bob Dylan, "Blowin' in the Wind";

"Scare a moose, scare a moose, will you do the banned tango?"
Queen, "Bohemian Rhapsody";

"Doodle like a lady!"
Aerosmith, "Dude (Looks like a Lady)";

"Shamu, the mysterious whale . . ."
U2, "Mysterious Ways"; and

"Here we are now, in containers!"
Nirvana, "Smells like Teen Spirit."

Hymn texts are also regularly misconstrued, especially by children learning the words by ear who are bewildered by theological vocabulary. Kissthisguy.com lists several texts of questionable theology that arise from these misunderstandings, like "Through many dangerous toys and snails I have already come" ("Amazing Grace"), "They are wheat but he is straw" ("Jesus Loves Me! This I Know"), and "Lead on, oh kinky turtle" ("Lead On, O King Eternal").

Listening and Hearing

Truth be told, I don't usually discuss misheard lyrics in the college music classes I teach (although this may change now that I've combed the side-splitting pages at Kissthisguy .com), but I do talk about the complex, multifaceted, and nuanced tasks of *listening* and *hearing*. What does it mean to listen well (besides hearing the intended lyrics correctly), and why might it be important to hone listening skills, even if you have no intention to pursue a career in music? What I attempt to demonstrate to my students, whether they are music majors or taking the class as part of their liberal arts core, is that music is much more than sounds, and that listening is a critical social and civic skill that can help us love our neighbors more fully. It may seem like a big leap from "mysterious whale" to brotherly love, but I think these misheard lyrics raise some pertinent questions about hearing (and mishearing) that might allow us to travel from the absurd to the profound.

To begin with, why and how are these misunderstood lyrics funny? Most readers of my (admittedly rather dated) examples above will laugh at the butchered lyrics from old hits that they know, but be puzzled by lyrics that are unfamiliar to them. Getting the joke requires inside knowledge about the music—you have to be able to hear how closely the inane lyric matches the real one in your head to be really delighted by it. In addition, we get special pleasure from hearing silly lyrics when the original ones are solemn, weighty, or passionate. Notice that all of the examples I cited come from songs considered "classics" in some way, and songs that take themselves very seriously—a civil rights song, a pop mini-opera, macho commentary on gender ambiguity, mystical reflections on love, an anthem of teenage angst, and earnest worship songs. Again, you need enough inside knowledge about the song, the artist, and the context to understand how deliciously irreverent the misheard lyric is. So already our misheard lyrics have brought us to an important insight about listening: when we listen to music (and musical parodies), we are divided into insiders and outsiders.

This kind of insider knowledge is at play in another wonderful misquoted lyric, "the ducks are hazards in the classroom," from the only radio hit of Pink Floyd's rock opera *The Wall*, "Another Brick in the Wall (Part 2)." The song is a protest against the harsh treatment of students in the British boarding school system, and the well-known chorus opens with "We don't need no education / We don't need no thought control." The subsequent line is supposed to be "No dark sarcasm in the classroom," but this lyric is routinely misunderstood to be about ducks, dogs, or dukes and their hazards, hassles, spasms, chasms, or castles. The image of ducks waddling through a boarding school classroom is amusing by itself, but like my other examples, the misunderstanding is especially funny when you have enough knowledge about the song to juxtapose this comic image with the utter seriousness with which *The Wall* was written in 1979. It is an 80-minute piece of musical theatre that chronicles the trials of an angst-ridden protagonist, Pink: his fatherless childhood, his overbearing mother, bullying at school, his failed marriage, and the emptiness he finds in rock-stardom and drug use. All of these painful episodes become metaphorical bricks in a psychological wall of isolation that Pink builds around himself. What's more, this elaborate narrative concept is set to music that is formally complex, stylistically diverse, dark in tone, and full of dramatic sound effects. These various artistic intricacies make it a model example of the progressive ("prog") rock genre of the 1970s, which strove to elevate rock 'n' roll above the status of "mere entertainment" to the more prestigious category of "art." While prog rock sometimes included strange and surreal imagery, insiders will immediately recognize that waddling ducks do not in fact belong in the grim inner world portrayed in *The Wall*.

For the legions who consider themselves fans of *The Wall* (it has sold an estimated 30 million copies worldwide), these insider details about the work are not trivial; they get to the very essence of the piece. The melodies of *The Wall* are catchy and the guitar solos impressive, yes, but equally compelling are the *ideas* behind it—that rock 'n' roll can be profound, epic, virtuosic, artistic, and smart. These qualities were seen at the time as an alternative to commercial, formulaic, fluffy radio hits with nothing to say, epitomized in the genres of bubblegum pop and disco. As is usually the case, here a new genre helped to define an "us" and a "them." Being a fan of Pink Floyd generally or *The Wall* specifically indicated a value judgment about what "good" art was. You could even argue that listening to "Another Brick in the Wall (Part 2)" without any understanding of what *The Wall* was trying to achieve in the pop culture battles of its day would be an even more profound mishearing of the work than thinking Roger Waters struggled with hazardous ducks in his childhood classrooms.

Cultural Baggage

What I'm getting at with my example from *The Wall* is that music has a lot of *cultural baggage* and that this cultural baggage is not superfluous to the music but is an integral part of how we hear and experience the music. My comments about progressive rock highlight how important genre categories are in how we think about music, and this is true for other genres besides progressive rock as well. Consider how offended a fan of "alternative" music might be if you called his music "pop," or consider how much you feel in common with someone you've met if you discover that she is a fan of blues / country / hip-hop / Baroque / electronica / Broadway show tunes—just like you—and you start to see that genre distinctions are usually perceived as distinctions of value, and that they are very important to us.

But music has a lot of other cultural baggage as well. In most of my introductory music courses I demonstrate this point by playing a series of unknown musical examples and asking the class to tell me about them. Amazingly, students are always able tell me a huge amount of cultural information about a short clip of music that they've never even heard before. If I play a hymn, they know it takes place in a church, is often associated with an older demographic, requires Sunday-best clothes or choir robes but not clapping, and is reverent and intended for worship. If I play jazz, they know it takes place in a club, is associated (historically) with African Americans, requires dressing up for a night on the town and clapping after solos, and is intended for relaxing, having fun, or dancing. If I play an opera clip, they know it takes place in an opera hall, is associated with an older, white, upper-class demographic, requires tuxes and gowns (traditionally) and sitting still without talking (with the exception of the occasional "Bravo!"), and is used to express drama and emotion. You get the idea. It turns out that in addition to communicating values and ideas associated with specific genres and pieces (as in my example from *The Wall*), music has the remarkable ability to communicate and suggest a lot of complex cultural information related to social groups, behavior, and function.

How exactly does music do this? One way is through the process of *enculturation*, which everyone undergoes by growing up in a culture and making connections and learning appropriate behaviors: you notice that mariachi music is played in Mexican restaurants, that people dance to hip-hop, and that it's OK to talk during jazz but not Beethoven. But perhaps an even more important way that music becomes so imbued with cultural meaning is through musical *discourse*, a fancy word that basically means everything we say about music, whether that be in conversations, history books, blogs, concert programs, classrooms, fan sites, CD covers, liner notes, reviews, lessons, rehearsals, advertisements, commentaries, or interviews. We often celebrate music's nonverbal qualities, its ability to speak without words, but it turns out that a lot of music's significance and power in our lives comes from stories about that music.

Some of these stories we tell about music are widely known and understood in the culture broadly; others are personal and highly specific. You might feel a sense of devotion in the music of Bach because you know he loved God, or, like me, you might find it soothing because your mother played it when you were young. You might have been drawn to Arcade Fire after reading a review commenting on the variety and complexity in their music, or because a Canadian friend told you it was a great band. You might get choked up hearing the hymn "Abide with Me" because of its comforting text and familiar form, or because it was your grandpa's favorite hymn before he died. You might scorn Justin Bieber because of his formulaic music and screaming fans, but be grudgingly impressed by his life story after your kid sister shows you clips of him playing the drums at age two. I didn't know anything about progressive rock when I first started listening to Pink Floyd, but I knew that they were an awesome band because they were a favorite of my brother, who was four-and-a-half years older and infinitely cooler than me. These examples show how much listening to music is also being part of a conversation about music. We are insiders and outsiders listening to music because we are in communities large and small that tell stories about music, and through these stories we learn to understand and love some kinds of music while being confused and repulsed by others.

What all of this suggests is that genuinely perceptive listening involves a lot more than just using our ears to take in melodies, rhythms, harmonies, instruments, and form in musical pieces, or even the lyrics and the worldviews they express. These structural and interpretive aspects of music are important, and I spend a lot of energy and time in my classes stretching students' ears to hear sounds and ideas in the music they hadn't discerned before. But you need to go a step further than this. To really hear a piece of music thoroughly, you also need to be attuned to the conversations about that piece and be able to distinguish and understand all its cultural baggage. It's this kind of humanistic listening to music, listening with ears ready to hear the people and communities behind the noise, that has the potential to help us love our neighbors more fully.

Music and Community

Still not convinced that enlightened listening might lead to love? To see how this might be so, you need to first understand that just as music has the ability to make people feel included, feel like part of a group of insiders, it also has the ability to make people feel excluded, feel like outsiders. Have you ever walked into a church and been so turned off by the music performed there that you couldn't worship? Have you ever been in a store and felt out of place because the music was obviously targeting a different demographic than yours? Have you ever fought with family members about which radio station to play in the car, or been driven insane by someone playing music you detested in your space? People often bond over music, but they fight about music a lot too. Why is that?

Let me take you back to that introductory lecture I described above, the one where I play unknown musical examples for students and ask them to tell me the setting, social group, behaviors, and attitudes associated with them. After I play a few familiar or recognizable genres (hymn, jazz, classical), I play a short *ganga* song from a remote highlander village in Bosnia. It features three women singing forcefully, almost shouting, in Bosnian. It starts with a short melody sung by one singer, and then two others join in, singing a full tone below the first singer to create very harsh dissonance. Finally, all the singers stop and join on a swooping up-and-down gesture that sounds a bit like a child shouting "Wheee!"

Students are always completely dumbfounded by this short piece. I ask them about the setting, social group, behaviors, and attitudes that this foreign music might be associated with, and all they can do is make wild guesses: African tribal ritual? Asian mourning song? Native American hunting call? They have no idea what genre the piece falls in, how you should behave while listening to it, how you would dress for it, what social group is associated with it, what the music means, whether it is stylish or outdated. If asked about the mood or emotion of the song, students usually guess that it is sad or angry. And they are shocked when I tell them that the text for the song means "Sisters, hold on to your chastity." What's going on here is that I've played a musical example outside of their community, and thus outside their musical discourse.

My listening experiment in class allows me to clarify something very important about music: although music is *universal* (found in all civilizations of all times and places around the world) and is in a way similar to *language* (a set of aural signs that allows you to communicate within a community), it is NOT a universal language. If it were, anyone anywhere in the world should be able to listen to a *ganga* song and intuit whether it was sad, happy, reverent, or playful. Your great-aunt should be able to listen to a screamo band and just "get it." But in fact, that's not what happens. The reality is that when we listen to music as outsiders (maybe because the music is from a different time, place, or demographic group), we all have tin ears. We all mishear to some degree. We fight about music because of these different ways of hearing. Listening to music without understanding its meaning in a given community is like listening to a foreign language you don't know—it sounds like gibberish and may be intriguing, boring, or annoying, depending on the context. In the same way that you wouldn't expect to listen to someone from Ghana speak Akan and understand it immediately, you shouldn't expect to listen to West African drumming and have it make sense to you without translation either. Or fifteenth-century Franco-Flemish polyphony. Or your cousin's annoying _____ album (insert genre or band that you absolutely cannot tolerate).

The reason this is such an important point (that music is not a universal language) is that it gets at the heart of how music unites us and divides us. Our own musical loves and biases become so familiar that they seem natural and obvious, and we start to expect everyone else to hear and think about music in the way we do. But the reality is that cultures and subcultures will listen to the same music and hear vastly different things. Part of being a proficient listener is understanding that other people will listen to music in a totally different way than you, and it will mean something different to them. For fans of progressive rock, for example, it seems simply self-evident that *of course* music that is more complicated and virtuosic is better. But what felt complex and deep to fans of *The Wall* in the late '70s felt silly and pretentious to others. It turns out that Pink Floyd fans came from quite a specific demographic—middle-class white males in their teens and early 20s. Lower-class white males of the same age group did not accept middle-class ideas about art (which were basically the values of classical music transferred onto rock) and instead began playing in a rough, rebellious, DIY style with little formal complexity, calling it punk. African Americans generally ignored progressive rock too, preferring danceable styles like funk and soul. For blacks in South Africa in the early 1980s, the single "Another Brick in the Wall (Part 2)" from *The Wall* had an entirely different association: because of its portrayal of boarding school abuses, it became a popular anti-Apartheid anthem and was eventually banned by ruling whites in that country. Later still, Germans used the music of *The Wall* to celebrate the fall of the Berlin Wall and the reunification of their country at a special live performance of the work in July 1990.

Is one of these ways of hearing *The Wall* the "correct" way to hear the album? Not in my classroom. In my class I'm far more interested in having you understand these different perspectives and listen from a position of humility. I want you to try to do the musical equivalent of walking a mile in your neighbor's shoes. This practice may help you love others by avoiding hateful stereotypes ("He listens to country, so he must be a redneck," "[Western] harmony is godly, [African] rhythm is pagan"), snap judgments ("No one can worship authentically to that music," "Chinese opera is not really music"), and sweeping generalizations ("Everyone who listens to metal participates in the occult," "All smart people like classical music"). It also might prompt you to think about your own music with the concerns of others in mind: Does my music make others feel uncomfortable, irritated, or excluded? Do others hear something different than I do in the music I love?

Given that music is a ubiquitous part of our daily experience and one of the most common ways people interact with each other (directly or indirectly), I would argue that learning to listen well is an important life skill. Music majors will hone this skill in sophisticated and complex ways, learning to understand and imitate a variety of styles and learning how to decipher and communicate musical meaning. But everyone, no matter their college major or occupation, should know how to listen so that they can at least avoid offending others in their musical activities. When listening is done with others in mind, it can indeed be a small way to love your neighbor.

Ducks may not be hazards in the classroom after all, but rather an invitation to listen with perception and grace.

Who Wants to Live in the "Real" World?

William Katerberg, History

Lexington, Massachusetts. April 1775.

Some seventy colonists face seven hundred soldiers in a skirmish that will start the American Revolution. The inexperienced rebels show courage as they line up on the commons to face the better-trained and much larger force. But when a shot rings out and the British regulars start firing, the rebel militia is quickly scattered, and the regulars march on to Concord, where, later that day, "the shot heard round the world" will be fired.

In an experiment, education professor Sam Wineburg had students and teachers read textbook accounts of the battle and examine primary records from the time. He was interested in how people think about the past. Professor Wineburg gave two drawings of the battle to Derek, one of the students in his experiment. He asked Derek to decide which drawing best fit with what the textbook and records revealed. One showed the colonists scattering, which fit with what Derek had read. But Derek picked the other drawing, which showed the colonists hiding behind trees, reloading their muskets and firing at the regulars. It would be crazy for them to stand out in the open and get shot, Derek explained to Wineburg.[1]

Derek's reasoning was logical, Wineburg observes, but wrong. Derek assumed that the colonists would fight as he would fight, as soldiers trained today would fight against superior forces. He didn't see what the records were telling him: the colonists stood in a line, out in the open, and were routed by the larger force of British regulars. He couldn't imagine them doing that. He didn't think to investigate the military practices of that time. Instead, he read the records of the battle, which seemed strange from his viewpoint, and revised them into something that made sense to him.

The example of Derek suggests that historical thinking is unnatural. It goes against the grain of how we think and act in our daily lives, where we assume that people—"normal" people, anyway—are pretty much like us. This is especially true when we think of our own nation or religious tradition. When we encounter people who seem strange, it's easy for us to dismiss them as stupid, crazy, or evil. Sometimes we cannot see how different people in the past were, so blinded are we by our own contemporary eyes. Understanding the past requires us to see both what is close to how we experience the world and what looks foreign and distant.

In one of my classes I have students read a book about the American family. It starts with families in the 1600s— Native American, Puritan, slave—and carries the story into our time.[2] The book shows how different families today are from those in the past: the function of the family in the community, the responsibilities of children, the roles of women and men, the place of the family within the structures of society. This study argues that the growth of individualism in American society in the 1800s and 1900s transformed families, particularly giving new opportunities to women as they gained legal equality and freedom. Families clearly are not eternally the same. They vary in significant ways from society to society, and they change over time. Not surprisingly, some people think changes in American family life have been good; others think they have been damaging.

As part of a writing assignment, I ask students to discuss whether they'd prefer to live as families did in the past, when the roles of women and men were more strictly defined, or as people do in the present, when individualism has made roles more interchangeable and fluid. Which would you choose? Most of my students choose present-day family life, but some choose the past. (As you might expect, more male students than female choose the past, when men had more power and women faced many constraints.) I ask students who say they'd prefer to live as families lived in the past whether they've thought about the fact that colleges had no female students. As women, they would not be here; as men, they'd have no women in their classes or on campus. Usually, none of them have thought about this. They know, intellectually, that as children they would be considered part of the family's workforce. They understand that as women they would have limited property rights and no voting rights. But they do not understand that the separate roles of women and men would mean that marriage relations would be far more formal than the easy give-and-take between the sexes to which they are accustomed. They do not realize how this profoundly different way of life would affect them and take away many things that they take for granted—such as women going to college and being able to choose a "traditional" women's role. Such things would no longer be choices but imposed. Students miss the fact that families in the 1600s should look strange to them, that their own lives would look to strange to people from the 1600s, and that something so basic to human existence as family life has changed significantly over four hundred years.

But so what? What good is training yourself to think historically? Why spend time in college learning to do it? I can give you lots of reasons: It will make you smarter, make you more money, and make you a better citizen. You might even enjoy doing it. But the most important reason is this: learning to put "reality" into question, to not take the world for granted, to understand that "reality" changes and that it can be changed—these are some of the most practical and hopeful things that you can discover. Let's start with the money.

A Desired Commodity for Industry

You can indeed make good money with a humanities degree. I have friends who studied history, as I did, but aren't teachers. They include business owners, speech writers for politicians, government bureaucrats, lawyers, pastors, and chefs.

My most financially-successful friend got a PhD in US history and wrote a book about the Vietnam War, but decided she didn't want to teach. She went into the business world instead and now works for a head-hunting firm. When big companies like GM or Ford, or large charities like the Red Cross need a new CEO, they hire a head-hunting firm. The firm does research on the organization—how it operates, its problems, its goals for the future. After helping the organization figure out what it needs, my friend helps her client find the right person for the job. Most of the people at my friend's head-hunting firm have degrees in business. Her bosses found that she did the job differently. She noticed things and had ideas that her colleagues with MBAs missed.[3] She was trained to think as a historian, not as a typical businessperson, and she brought that perspective to her job. She quickly climbed the corporate ladder and became a partner in her firm. She finds her job intellectually stimulating and rewarding, makes lots of money, and has no regrets about studying history.

Need more convincing? Recently it was reported that tech firms like Google are hiring people with degrees in disciplines such as philosophy, literature, and history. "You go into the humanities to pursue your intellectual passion," explains Damon Horowitz, "and it just so happens, as a by-product, that you emerge as a desired commodity for industry. Such is the halo of human flourishing."[4]

Horowitz is director of engineering for Google, specializing in artificial intelligence (AI) research; he is one of the company's "in-house philosophers." AI work was getting nowhere, he found, producing clever computers but nothing like human consciousness. This raised questions about what it means to be human. Horowitz thought he might better understand how to pursue AI—and make gobs of money for Google and himself—if he and other engineers and marketers at Google started to do some philosophizing about what it means to be human.

These companies have started hiring graduates trained in the humanities, thousands and thousands of them.

So there you have it. Become a desired commodity for industry and flourish as a person. But there's more.

They Weren't So Stupid . . . and Neither Are You

It's easy for us to view people in the past as barbaric because of what they believed or how they lived. Perhaps some were. *Perhaps we are.* We should remember that many aspects of our lives will appear monstrous from the viewpoint of people looking back at us a century from now. Think about it. What do you believe or do that people in the future will judge bizarre or immoral? Will it be the way we accept high concussion rates among football and hockey players because we like violent sports? The way we sexualize all aspects of life and put them on display on television? The inequalities gay and lesbian people face? Our worship of wealth? The way we use up resources, pile on debt, and produce pollution like there's no tomorrow? These things are commonplace today. How will future societies judge us on these matters? It might be none of these things—issues that we debate and fight over today, depending on our politics, values, and tastes. But that's the point. It's hard for us to envision a society so different from our own, including our own society in the future, that we can't imagine how people then will view many aspects of life that seem normal and unremarkable for us. (Now you're starting to think historically, about yourself and your own society.)

Another goal of historical thinking is to understand people on their own terms. This does not require us to accept earlier thinking about how life should be lived as good or true, but simply to set aside, temporarily, our own ways and expectations so that we might try to think and feel our way into theirs. Take an extreme example. How did it come to seem normal and morally proper in some parts of Indian society to practice sati, the ritual burning of many of a prominent man's possessions when he died—including his wife? In early nineteenth-century India sati was not widespread, but each year dozens of women chose, or were forced, to immolate themselves. Here's an example that may be closer to home: imagine what it would be like to live in a society in which children start to work like adults at the age of ten or twelve, as was true in America and in Europe well into the 1800s (and is still true today in some parts of the world).

But what is the value of learning to see differences in how people from other societies or cultures understand the world from their point of view, not your own, and to resist judging them as stupid, insane, or evil? What is the use of understanding that people from other traditions might see us as barbaric?

Think of it as the "long route" to the self.[5] None of us becomes who we are on our own, solely by looking inside and finding ourselves. We become who we are through our encounters with other people, experiencing how they are different; in those encounters, we recognize things about ourselves. Sometimes we imitate others, learning from them and adapting their ways. Other times we reject things about them and cultivate in ourselves different sensibilities and practices. Some of this is conscious, but most of it happens without us even noticing what we're doing or thinking. This is true not just of our relationships with our parents, sisters and brothers, relatives, and friends; it is true also of our encounters with strangers—people from different cultural traditions or nations—whether we meet them on TV, as a family that moves in next door, as classmates at university, or as tourists. This adaptation is true not only of day-to-day things like clothing, food, and social customs, but also of the values we hold about things like politics, religious practices, and family life. Other people and their ways play a vital role in shaping who we are; we, in turn, shape them.

We experience something similar when we study the past. We don't encounter people in written records in the same direct way as we do people in daily life, but we can learn about how they lived and viewed the world. We can read their letters, diaries, novels, poetry, legal documents,

49

business records, and spiritual writings. This is true about people from our own past (say, American and Christian) or from the past in other societies and traditions (say, Iranian and Muslim).

When we study the past in this way, we learn that life and people have been different. Other subjects within the humanities explore differences between societies and traditions too (literature, religious studies, cultural anthropology), but history especially shows how ways of life in a society—such as how families work—can change dramatically. These changes can be for good or ill. But things do change.

Understanding that this is true of both others and ourselves—that we should not dismiss people who are different and that they shouldn't dismiss us—has a humanizing effect and teaches humility. It's a way of following the command in the Hebrew and Christian Scriptures to love our neighbors as ourselves. By learning to see both the strange and the familiar in our neighbors, both those next door and those around the world, and by remembering that they similarly find us strange, we learn to see others as human and not as enemies or monsters. We also come understand our own humanity better, learning to see ourselves as strange rather than familiar. The humanities teach us the habits of this kind of seeing.

The Hope of the Past

People sometimes say to those who have ideas they think impractical, "You need to deal with the real world." People usually mean well when they say this. They're half right. As individuals, we cannot always change how the world works. Neither is it helpful to respond with cynicism or to rebel in self-destructive ways. We need to adapt to the society around us in ways that are practical and don't compromise us morally so that perhaps we can change some small things about our circumstances.

In the long run, though, this advice is limiting. Learning the habit of realism is dangerous. It can lead to complacency or despair—so that we never try to change things—or it can lead us to assume that our way of life is as good as it gets. And as we've seen, for good or for ill, things do change. It's not just that there are differences between societies; societies themselves change over time.

White American Christians once thought that non-white people and women were essentially different from white men and women—naturally and biologically different—and shouldn't have the same rights. They owned black people and felt free to rape them, sell them, and separate parents and children. Slaves had a legal status little different from animals. A century ago in parts of the United States, it was publicly acceptable to lynch a black man on the simple accusation of a white person—beating, hanging, shooting, even castrating a black man, burning his body while crowds watched and photographers took postcard pictures of the corpse. The church-going people and government officials who participated in these events believed that the social order that justified lynching was ordained by God. But in 2008 the United States elected an African American president.

Things change, basic things. A century and a half ago, women were barred from most universities and professions. Today there are more women in US colleges and universities than men. Racism and sexism have not disappeared, nor has civil violence. But although many people once considered it natural, legal, and morally right to discriminate against people of color and women, few would argue that point today.

Thus, one of the most useful things that studying history can impart is hope. This might sound strange, especially if your history teacher is a cynic who only points out the awful things in history. But hope depends on the possibility that life can change, especially for people who suffer from oppression or inequality, or the terrors of war, poverty, disease, or natural disaster. History makes no promise that things will get better; sometimes, things will get worse. But those who say that life is what it is and insist that we should accept reality as it is are ignoring what history teaches. They are choosing to accept the status quo for what it is, for practical reasons, because they've lost hope that things can be different, or because they benefit from the status quo. But things do change, and not just small things.

This insight isn't unique to historical study, but it is an insight that has encouraged those who recognize the influence that the past has on us. Therapists help people with emotional difficulties, often from traumas in the past, to deal with their problems and change so they can live in more fulfilling ways in the future. Christian activists like Martin Luther King Jr. believed that God is working in history and that God's people are partners in the story of God's kingdom. Memories of God's faithfulness in their own history, echoing stories of the exodus and the promised land in the Bible, gave civil rights activists hope, spurring their resistance against the segregated society in which they lived. During the 1960s, when civil rights workers were imprisoned and beaten, when equality for African Americans seemed far away, the hope that things can change, sometimes for the better, remained alive. It's not a liberal or a conservative lesson, or unique to the civil rights movement, but one understood by activists of every stripe.

History for Life

"I want to show how different the past was," Natalie Zemon Davis said when asked why she was a historian. "I want to show that even when times were hard, people found ways to cope . . . and maybe resist it. I want people today to be able to connect with the past by looking at the tragedies and the sufferings of the past, the cruelties and the hatefulness, the hope of the past, the love the people had, and the beating that they had. They sought for power over each other, but they helped each other, too. They did things both out of love and fear. . . . Especially I want to show that it could be different, that it was different, and that there are alternatives."[6]

Reality changes, and we shape that process for good or for ill as individuals and societies. This knowledge is a key component of hope and should spur us to action. Studying the humanities and cultivating a critical yet hopeful questioning of reality is a viable road to the good life in all its forms, from riches to a better understanding of oneself and others. It's part of "the halo of human flourishing," as Google's philosopher-programmer Damon Horowitz put it.

But what does human flourishing amount to? Can you find the answer in a Google search? That flourishing includes the potential for interesting and even lucrative jobs in a variety of fields, including working for Horowitz and making Google search algorithms sing. But the humanities also give us the skills and inclination to go deeper than a Google search. For example, they encourage us to take a close look at Google itself. Should we admire it for its commitment to delivering many of the classic texts of celebrated

53

thinkers and writers for free online—from Aristotle and St. Augustine to Karl Marx, Mary Shelley, and Mark Twain? Or should we be wary of its commercial motives, as every search leads to an opportunity to shop?

If there is one genuine lesson, one piece of wisdom, that historical thinking and the humanities impart, it is this: do not be complacent.

How much more practical can it get?

Notes

1. Sam Wineburg, "Historical Thinking and Other Unnatural Acts," *Phi Delta Kappan* 80, no. 7 (March 1999): 481–94.

2. Steven Mintz and Susan Kellogg, *Domestic Revolutions: A Social History of American Family Life* (New York: The Free Press, 1989).

3. In the *Harvard Business Review* blog, Tony Golsby-Smith makes the same point: "Want Innovative Thinking? Hire from the Humanities," March 31, 2011, http://blogs.hbr.org /cs/2011/03/want_innovative_thinking_hire.html (accessed June 21, 2011).

4. Quoted in Matthew Reisz, "Google leads search for humanities PhD graduates," *The Times Higher Education*, http://www .timeshighereducation.co.uk/story.asp?storycode=416190 (accessed May 31, 2011).

5. Richard Kearney, *On Paul Ricoeur: The Owl of Minerva* (Aldershot, UK: Ashgate, 2004).

6. Interview with Natalie Zemon Davis in Henry Abelove et al., eds., *Visions of History* (Manchester, UK: Manchester University Press, 1984), 114–15.

Getting Engaged
The Joys of Studying History

Karin Maag, History

To put their customers at ease, hairstylists often make small-talk. I always do my best to respond, both because I like chatting with them and because they are wielding sharp scissors near my neck and ears. One favorite question I get asked is "So what do you do?" When I reply that I teach college-level history, I often get the following response: "Oh . . . I hated history in school. It was my worst subject because it was so boring . . . All that memorizing." This is a discouraging starting point for further conversation, but it does offer me a chance to discuss how we can learn about the past, especially at the college level, and it gives me an opportunity to make the case for history as both an exciting and rewarding field of study for college students.

If you are fascinated by the stories of the past, you already have a great starting point as a history major. But unlike some students' experience of high school history, the point is not to memorize long lists of unconnected facts, names, and dates in preparation for multiple-choice tests. In fact, students who excelled in memorization in high school history classes and expected to do equally well in their college-level history classes sometimes struggle, because the emphasis now is less on learning facts and more on making connections. Although chronological reference points are still fundamental, the aim is more to use these as anchors for analysis and persuasive argument. Understanding why events happened and how these occurrences fit together and influence each other is key. Watching students gain confidence in their ability to analyze historical events and make connections over the course of their time as history majors is akin to watching novice climbers tackle the climbing wall in our campus sports center: they learn not only to use various handholds and footholds, but also to plot out routes and use the holds to make their way to the top.

A Reshaping Experience

So why should you seriously consider becoming a history major at college? Somewhere along the line, you may have heard a saying about the purpose of history, something like "Those who don't study the past are doomed to repeat it." The quotation comes from American philosopher George Santayana, who actually said, "Those who cannot remember the past are condemned to repeat it." You could use Santayana's statement to make the case that history is important for the lessons it can teach about how to handle current problems. If we do not study the past and learn from it, we are likely to make the same mistakes as previous generations did when confronting similar issues.

However, this largely utilitarian approach stops well short of providing a deeper understanding into why history matters. What is missing is any sense that at its best, studying history is a transformative and reshaping experience, an experience that can lead to a new and larger understanding of human motivations, both at the individual and community level, and a new or renewed commitment to an active and engaged life. The study of history is vital to undergraduate education. Even a single history course can transform your entire worldview, because it calls us unapologetically to engagement in the contemporary world.

Fostering Critical Thinking

One of the chief assets a student of history develops is a nimble mind. A history major learns in depth about the ways in which people in the past tackled the challenges they faced, and about their stories of triumphs and struggles. But the nimble mind of the historian makes connections between events and across cultures, weighing similarities and differences, considering what changed and what remained the same, comparing the approaches taken to similar problems.

Once you understand, for instance, how the ancient Chinese schools of thought known as Confucianism, Taoism, and Legalism gave competing solutions to the troubles generated by the Period of the Warring States in China and its aftermath (c. 403–221 BC), you can compare the responses and analyze the strengths and weaknesses of each school. Confucianism advocated living a life of service to one's neighbor and one's government, and focused on education and ethical instruction as the best tools to restore order. The Taoists, for their part, felt that the best strategy was to withdraw from the conflicts and focus on internal harmony, peace, and creative inaction. The Legalists (whose views were in fact adopted by the Qin dynasty, which restored order) were strong proponents of using tough laws and harsh punishments to ensure stability and maintain peace in society. However, there was a high cost to this strategy: anyone who stood in the way was eliminated, books were burned, and over four hundred scholars were buried alive for their opposition to the new regime. Analyzing both the problems (endemic fighting, lack of security, and a breakdown of social order) and the competing solutions (highly ethical activism, withdrawal to focus on the inner life, or strongly authoritarian government action) allows you to gain an understanding of the complexity inherent in addressing social turmoil in the ancient world.

The student of history, in this analysis, comes to realize that no one solution worked perfectly, that each had its downsides, and that the way forward lay in adopting the best characteristics of each school of thought. It is this kind of analysis that helps the student of history to work in assessing contemporary challenges that have some similarities, such as current government struggles to balance national budgets or restore order after a period of social revolution. What possible solutions to these problems can be articulated, and what are the strengths and weaknesses of each strategy?

Learning Empathy

College-level history classes can challenge apathy and self-interest by confronting students with the costs of self-interest in the past. You will learn about major crises in world history, including revolutions, wars, and epidemics. And you will learn what happens in a society when people avoid getting involved while someone else is mistreated, or when they choose to look away while a person or a group is being targeted by the powerful, or when they put their own well-being ahead of providing assistance to their neighbors. Again and again, we note how acts of human violence against others are facilitated by the willingness of the majority to close their eyes to what is happening.

Students in my classes often come to grips with the costs and consequences of inaction and disengagement when they take part in role playing. Let's imagine you are a participant.

You pick a piece of paper out of a bag on your way into class. Each slip of paper indicates the name of a particular group or occupation. The year is 1347, and the Black Death has begun to surface in your town. In groups of four or five, you and your classmates become the town's government officials, merchants, physicians, clergy, parents with young children, beggars, and Jews. Each group is asked to decide what they will do in the face of the advancing epidemic. What would you do? Often, as students get caught up in their roles, they give very pragmatic or self-preserving responses, ones that first and foremost would ensure the survival and safety of their own group and their own families. Fleeing the town to some other perceived place of safety is always a popular option. In many instances, the beggars and the Jews get blamed for being the carriers of the disease and are compelled to leave town or are forcibly quarantined. When confronted with particular situations, such as an older neighbor with worrying symptoms, the students want to have as little contact with the possible victim of the plague as they can. They do not want to get involved in other people's problems if such actions would put their own health or that of their families at risk.

When the role playing is done, we discuss the various groups' responses, taking time to examine them in the light of faith commitments. Different reactions begin to surface. Students become powerfully aware of the disconnect between what they profess and how they react in a crisis situation. If their own key interest in times of crisis lies in saving themselves and their families with only minimal concern for those around them, and if scapegoating the vulnerable is their first response, students begin to realize more acutely how these same pressures could have affected people in the past and led to serious social turmoil. Their tendency to make snap judgments about people's decisions in the past is replaced by a deeper sense of the stark choices these people faced. This classroom experience confronts Christian students with the costs of following Christ's teaching to love their neighbors.

Hearing the Voices of the Past

Believe it or not, you have primary sources in your wallet. Your ID, bank cards, membership cards, family photos, and cash all situate you in a specific time and place. Based on what's in your wallet, a historian can learn a great deal about you as an individual and about your society. For historians, primary sources are texts, images, or artifacts created by those who witnessed or participated in a given event or time period in the past. These primary sources are the lifeblood of history.

Sometimes the smallest fragments from human history can tell us a great deal about a particular time period and the challenges people faced at that time, just like the currency in your wallet. In my history classes, I often pull out a coin and pass it around. It is a small, silver-colored coin. The first thing students notice is how light the coin is, and then they see the date: 1943. They quickly deduce that the coin is made of some inexpensive lightweight metal, probably tin, given wartime restrictions on the use of more precious metals usually used in coinage. I then ask the class to figure out the language on the coin so that we can establish where it was made. Someone usually correctly identifies the language as French. So we have a very lightweight French coin from 1943.

We then turn to the words on the coin. I first ask if anyone knows the current motto of France, in use since the French Revolution. Again, one or more students know that the motto is *Liberté, Egalité, Fraternité,* or "Liberty, Equality, Fraternity." I explain that France's motto normally appears on official buildings and on its currency, just as "In God We Trust" appears on US currency (on coinage starting in 1864, and on bills starting in 1957). But the "Liberty, Equality, Fraternity" motto does not appear on the 1943 coin. Instead, the three words that do appear are *Travail, Famille, Patrie* ("Work, Family, and Fatherland"). As a class, we then discuss why the motto was changed on World War II–era French currency, and I remind the students about the fate of France following the Nazi attack in the spring of 1940: the northern section was occupied, whereas the southern part remained officially "free" but in reality under Nazi control until the whole country was occupied by the Germans late in 1942. Over the course of the discussion, students come to realize the power of the "Liberty, Equality, Fraternity" motto as a rallying point for French citizens who wanted to be free from Nazi rule, and the reasons why the French government that at the time more or less willingly collaborated with the Nazis consciously picked a much less potent and much more conservative motto for its currency.

If you were in this class, this small coin would show you something of the tensions and challenges facing a country under occupation or precariously trying to maintain some measure of autonomy in the face of constant pressure. You would have a chance to reflect on the values that you support and express freely, and you might get a sense for what it would be like if a war made it unsafe to display your values in public, even on the face of a coin. Your understanding of what life under foreign occupation might mean could grow by leaps and bounds, simply by passing around and analyzing one small and seemingly insignificant object.

Wisdom for the Present

Although primary sources need to be analyzed carefully and are not to be taken only at face value, they do provide the best route to learning how people at the time understood a given event. In all history classes at the college level, you will spend a considerable amount of time reading, discussing, and analyzing a range of primary sources. We repeatedly practice presenting the context, summarizing the content, and analyzing the significance of the primary sources we encounter. Most students come into introductory-level courses able to summarize the content of primary sources fairly effectively, but few are proficient at the start at incorporating analysis of the context and significance of the source. Considering the author's reasons for writing, depicting, or creating an artifact, as well as the potential audience and genre of the source, are all skills that most students need to develop.

As you work on these core abilities, you increasingly make connections between the topics addressed by the sources and the ways in which these same issues are tackled today. For instance, after reading and reflecting on the sixth-century Rule of Saint Benedict and the thirteenth-century Rule of Saint Francis for the religious communities these two church leaders established, one student began making important connections in her weekly reading report. As she analyzed the ways in which these religious communities ordered their priorities, she compared what she was learning to her own religious practices. She highlighted how the Rule of Saint Benedict called for a genuine commitment to putting one's faith at the center of one's life and noted that in contrast, it seemed to her that her own life of faith was more superficial and focused on being happy rather than addressing the challenges of following Christ. She questioned whether the young adult expressions of faith she saw in the dorm and campus community were grounded enough to deal honestly with doubt, for example. In a fruitful way, this student's comparison of two medieval texts helped her explore and better understand her own faith practice.

Reconsidering Our Preconceptions

Reading and discussing primary source texts in class can also awaken students to the realization that what they previously have absorbed from their surrounding culture about a given group of people or period of history might not be accurate. In the core survey course covering the period from earliest human history to 1500, one of the topics covered is the rise and spread of Islam. If I say the word "Islam" to you, what images come to your mind? Students in my class get the opportunity to read translated extracts of the Qur'an and of the Hadith (the sayings of the prophet Muhammad). In many ways, these are challenging readings, not so much because of their style but because of their content. Students are confronted by the fact that many passages of the Qur'an uphold strong ethical values, including the obligation to care for widows, orphans, and the poor. We learn about the Five Pillars of Islam and consider the importance Islam places on living a devout and charity-oriented life. As students wrestle with these texts, weighing the passages that advocate violence against the passages that speak of peace, they realize that the undifferentiated picture of Islam often presented in the Western media does not do justice to the complexities of this faith. As they become more knowledgeable, they recognize that they have to take seriously their responsibility to share what they have learned with those around them, to address stereotypes and dispel uninformed misconceptions.

The study of history can make you see the world through different eyes. You learn to think critically, to make connections, to consider audience and authorial intent when analyzing primary sources, to develop empathy with past generations, and to combat apathy and misconceptions—both your own and those of others around you. Each of these goals is not necessarily unique to history classes; other courses across the college focus on many of these same skills, but history courses ably address all of them. Studying history gives you a renewed sense of the importance of your engagement in this world.

And there is nothing boring about that!

Good Looking

Henry Luttikhuizen, Art History

> The true mystery of the world is the visible, not the invisible.
> —Lord Henry, in Oscar Wilde's *The Picture of Dorian Gray*

> You can observe a lot by watching.
> —Yogi Berra, Hall of Fame baseball player

Visual images help human beings find things out. They enable us to solve numerous problems. Travelers read road maps or look at their GPS to see where they are going (or, at least, should be going). Doctors look at medical pictures, such as CAT scans, x-rays, and ultrasounds, to discover what is happening inside their patients' bodies. Police search for visual clues to solve a crime. The interpretation of visual images is closely linked to our desire to know.

But sometimes, when I am looking for something, I have difficulty finding it, even when it is right smack in front of me. Eyeglasses, car keys, and wallet periodically elude me. Although it might seem more comforting to think these items have walked away all by their lonesome, on nearly every occasion they were lost because I had failed to pay attention. Simply put, I forgot where I had left them, so they became misplaced. My guess is that I am not alone. We all have our moments. These lapses may be frustrating, but they remind us just how dependent we are on memory and sight.

The power of sight affects us every day: we look both ways before we cross the street, we keep our eye on the ball, we watch out for falling rocks—but we rarely think about what it means to see. One of the advantages of the college humanities curriculum is that it offers us opportunities to think more carefully about ways of seeing.

Our Vision Is More Than Biological

Though we cannot look at anything without our eyes, our vision is more than biological. Cultural expectations also play a major role in what we see and how we see it. They help to shape how visual images are made and how they are perceived. If this were not the case, there would be no history of visual images. But people do look at the world in different ways, and one of the reasons to study art history is to understand how and why this is the case. To put it briefly, art history helps us to see things in context.

Let me give you a few examples. Imagine drawing a heart. My guess is that your imagined heart has a double arch on the top and comes to a single point at the bottom. This is the standard way we represent hearts. We anticipate that loved ones will send us Valentine's Day cards with hearts in this shape and that they expect the same from us. However, when we visit a cardiologist's office, we hope the doctor does not view hearts the same way. After all, human hearts do not resemble the typical way we represent them. So why do we draw them in this distorted manner? The answer lies in history.

Silphium, a now-extinct plant from North Africa, had seedpods that were what we would call heart-shaped. In ancient Egypt, seeds from this plant were used as contraceptives. Not surprisingly, the shape became associated with sexual interest. But that is not the whole story.

In the Old Testament, it is stated that the Word of God should be written in our hearts. According to tradition, Moses received the Ten Commandments on two tablets. One interpretation holds that the first tablet listed rules concerning love for God; the second one focused on how we should love our neighbors. Since the Middle Ages, the heart shape was believed to unify the two tablets into one symbol for love. The importance of the shape was reinforced by the notion that we memorize by heart. In Latin, to record (*recordari*) is literally to return memories back to the heart (*cordis*). Consequently, it has become commonplace to remember our loved ones with heart-shaped images that do not look like human hearts.[1]

My point is not to insist that we need to redraw hearts so that they correspond better with human anatomy, but to illustrate what art historians do. We investigate what visual images look like and why they look that way. For some, this might seem like an intellectual parlor game, analogous to playing Jeopardy or Trivial Pursuit. However, it is much more than that.

Art history helps us to understand human behavior. Every culture makes use of visual images. They play significant roles, and yet they do not all look the same or function in the same way from one culture to the next. This is not merely a matter of artistic skill. On the contrary, it is deeply tied to specific cultural expectations: paintings, sculptures, and visual arts of all types are produced because they are believed to be worth having. One of the things that art historians try to figure out is why these objects were made. Analyzing the visual appearance of these items can help us to understand not only what people have done but also what they hoped to accomplish.

Art history is important because it fosters greater empathy. It teaches us things about the beliefs and practices of distant peoples, those removed from us in historical time and geographical space. In a sense, it brings other human beings closer to us by showing us what they might have wanted and how they communicated their desires. In a world increasingly interconnected by digital communication, understanding the ideas and practices of others has gained greater importance. We can no longer afford to be naive about non-Western cultures; studying art history can help us to remedy this problem.

At the same time, art history can teach us about ourselves. It can make us more self-conscious about the way we do things. We draw hearts in a particular manner because it seems to have worked well in the past and will hopefully communicate our desires well in the present. Otherwise, we would look for a different visual strategy. Knowing the history of this practice will not improve one's ability to draw hearts. Nonetheless, it will enhance one's capacity to see the meaning of the shape, and it will help us to understand why we continue to render hearts in this particular way.

Visual Images and Historical Context

To understand images, it is vital to consider their historical contexts. Without that context, we are prone to misinterpret. Many readers of Dan Brown's *The Da Vinci Code* (as well as viewers of the subsequent film) take the author at his word and believe that the figure adjacent to Christ in Leonardo da Vinci's *Last Supper* is Mary Magdalene. Although this view may be intriguing within the story line, it carries no historical weight. Sorry to ruin the mystery or break the code, but there is no reason to believe that the figure in question is anyone other than the Apostle John, who is often shown next to Jesus as a young effeminate man. Interpreting art demands a close attention to visual details as well as a careful analysis of a piece's historical setting.

Consider the painting reproduced on the next page. At first glance, this painting may seem quite straightforward. It shows a man and a woman with a goldsmith in his shop. As we look more closely at the painting, however, it becomes more intriguing—and more meaningful. On the bottom of the picture is an inscription; translated into English, it reads, "Master Petrus Christus made me in the year 1449." This tells us who made it and when. But there is an enigmatic mark after the text. Petrus Christus has placed a heart symbol combined with parts from a mechanical clock next to the inscription. What does this mean? Is it is a personal insignia, or does it relate to the goldsmith or his customers? Unfortunately, art historians have yet to figure this out. It remains a mystery.

The customers, who are in the process of selecting a wedding ring, seem quite wealthy. She is wearing an opulent dress; her expensive bridal girdle can be seen on the counter. He is also quite fashionable in his attire, grasping the tip of his ceremonial sword and wearing a necklace with a pendant showing the coat of arms of the duke of Guelders. Nonetheless, there is insufficient evidence to identify him. Although the couple appears to be preparing for marriage, there is no record of a ducal wedding in 1449. The figures may be nothing more than a representation of ideal customers. Or they may be actual persons.

Even more puzzling, the goldsmith's face received more attention from the artist than those of the customers. Recent

Petrus Christus. *A Goldsmith in His Shop.* 1449. Oil on oak panel, 38⅝ × 33¾ in. Robert Lehman Collection, The Metropolitan Museum of Art, New York. With permission of Art Resource, New York.

infrared studies have revealed underdrawings suggesting that Petrus Christus was preoccupied with rendering the qualities of the goldsmith's face in meticulous detail. So the painting might be a portrait. But a portrait of whom? For well over a century it was assumed that the figure represents Saint Eloy, otherwise known as Saint Eligius, the patron saint of goldsmiths. This interpretation was thrown into doubt when conservators determined that a halo painted over the goldsmith's head was not part of the original composition (they removed it in 1993). Still, fifteenth-century Flemish and Dutch painters commonly represented holy figures without halos, so we cannot completely rule out the man's saintly status. We are simply uncertain about whether he is Eloy, or an unidentified goldsmith, or perhaps a figure alluding to both.

All of this adds to the mystery of the image, for we cannot tell whether we are looking at a portrait, a devotional painting, or both simultaneously. The panel opens up lots of questions. Are we enjoying a glimpse of something sacred, or are we merely encountering a mundane event rendered as if it were holy? Do we ever collapse the sacred and the secular? Is this a wise practice?

Since the picture is visually complex and invites personal reflection, one might expect it to be intimate and therefore small in size. The panel, however, is quite large, measuring nearly a square yard. The half-length figures are life-size in scale. This makes it seem as if we are sharing the same space with them. The scale of the image suggests that it was probably displayed in a prominent location, perhaps the goldsmith guild's chapel in Bruges. But without documentation, we cannot say for sure.

Despite the many things that remain unknown about this fifteenth-century painting, it encourages us to think more carefully about the relationship between sight and desire. The shelves behind the goldsmith are filled with items associated with his craft. On the top shelf, a set of *present-kannen*, highly polished pewter pitchers frequently given by aldermen to prominent guests at important civic occasions, can be seen. A string of prayer beads and an exquisite belt buckle hang from nails pounded into the upper shelf. The lower shelf, covered with white linen, is also loaded with expensive goods: open black pouches revealing seed pearls and other precious gems, a block of crystal and another of porphyry, a set of finely crafted broaches. There is also an open box on the shelf, revealing numerous gold rings with gemstones. The crystalline vessel above the box is a reliquary monstrance, a container meant to hold the consecrated host (that is, the body and blood of Christ in the appearance of an unleavened wafer). Like the *presentkannen*, the monstrance not only advertises luxurious goods; it also shows the goldsmith's service to the community and the Church.

The lower shelf also contains items associated with protection from poison. The branch of red coral was believed to have the power to defend its wearer against the evil eye and sterility. The fossilized shark teeth, called "serpent tongues" by contemporaries, hanging on a nail above the coral and mixed with the precious stones in an open black sack, were believed to change color when dipped in toxic food or drink. Finally, drinking from a chalice made of coconut shell, such as the one displayed on the left side of the shelf, was believed to provide an antidote to poison. Once again, these items reveal the value of the goldsmith's goods beyond their material worth.

The goods displayed in the goldsmith's shop appear to be finely crafted, enhancing their desirability. As viewers and potential customers, we tend to appreciate exquisitely produced items made out of precious materials. These objects seem to be worth more than those produced with less skill and with cheaper materials. However, once again, the painting asks us questions. What is the relationship between material and spiritual values? Do they necessarily conflict with one another? Do we have to choose one option over the other? If not, how do you find the proper balance between these values?

On the right side of the table, a convex mirror is depicted. Not only does the mirror show another example of the gold-smith's handiwork; it also reflects part of the cityscape outside the shop's interior. Part of the goldsmith's red cloak and part of the building (the door jamb or window casing) are reflected on the mirror's edges, subtly uniting the shop with the neighborhood. The reflection also includes a couple of dandies, a falconer and his colleague, peeking at the scene from outside. Although falconers are sometimes associated with the hunt or pursuit of courtly love, in this context he is likely a suggestion of envy or greed. A closer examination of the mirror reveals that it is cracked and spotted. Damaged by vice, the men do not appear to see the true value of the expensive items displayed. They seem to lust after the precious objects they see in the shop.

By contrast, the couple in the shop seems aware of a deeper meaning in the material. Embracing the woman with his right arm, the man watches the goldsmith weighing the ring to ensure honesty. In addition, he seems to be contemplating whether the ring is worthy enough to communicate his love and devotion. Meanwhile, his fiancée reaches toward the scales, implying that the ring is sufficient in value to indicate his commitment. The goldsmith's balance tips to his right, suggesting that the couple's love and virtue outweigh the sentiments of the men reflected in the mirror.[2]

Cultivating Empathy

Petrus Christus's painting is itself *exquisitely* designed and costly. In Bruges, painters belonged to the same guild as goldsmiths. Petrus Christus likely shared beliefs about sight and desire with the person or persons who commissioned his painting. His painting shows the value of fine craftsmanship, but it also reminds viewers that there are things in this world more important than monetary worth. His panel encourages us to ponder the meaning of vocation. Although the development of technical skills may be crucial for making a good living, there is a bigger picture he asks us to consider.

Most of the students in my art history courses are not going to become art historians and museum curators. Nor will you see them on television, assessing the worth of items on the *Antiques Roadshow* or the like. Nonetheless, art history is valuable for everyone who studies it. We live in a world filled with visual images that elicit response. In our culture, a picture is worth a thousand words, and we see lots of them every day. Even though we may not be aware of the power visual images play in our lives, they can and do affect us in profound ways. If that were not the case, no company would spend millions on a thirty-second Super Bowl ad. The power of pictures extends far beyond the art museum or gallery. It is important for us to understand how they work.

Images can be captivating, but studying visual practices is not merely a matter of idle fascination or vain curiosity. On the contrary, visual images offer us opportunities to learn more about human thoughts, desires, and actions. Interpreting visual images demands sensitivity to historical distance and difference. Yet without the gesture of empathy, we will likely fail to see why human artifacts look the way they do. Nor will we likely be able to understand how they have affected those who have viewed them. Simply put, we need to care about what we are seeing and recognize the value of studying it. Examining the history of art can help us to do that.

Notes

1. For more on the metaphor of the heart, see Eric Jager, *The Book of the Heart* (Chicago: University of Chicago Press, 2001).

2. For more on the Petrus Christus painting, see Bret Rothstein, *Sight and Spirituality in Early Netherlandish Painting* (Cambridge: Cambridge University Press, 2005), 1–10; Hugo van der Velden, "Defrocking St. Eloy: Petrus Christus's Vocational Painting of a Goldsmith," *Simiolus* 26 (1998): 242–76; Maryan Ainsworth, *Petrus Christus, Renaissance Master of Bruges: Exhibition Catalogue* (New York: The Metropolitan Museum of Art, 1994), 96–101; and Peter Schabacker, "Petrus Christus's Saint Eloy: Problems of Provenance, Sources and Meaning," *Art Quarterly* 35 (1972): 103–20.

Science in a Human Matrix

Matthew Walhout, Interdisciplinary Studies of Science

Recently several students showed up early for the history of science class I was teaching. This was a capstone course for juniors and seniors majoring in the physical sciences, so these students had a lot of chemistry, physics, and geology under their belts. Though it was only 8:30 in the morning, they seemed eager to discuss the assigned reading. The conversation began like this:

Cathy: "I feel cheated! Why didn't they teach us any of this in our science classes?"

Rachel: "Probably because it would take our minds off of the important scientific stuff."

Cathy: "Wait, what do you mean by *important*? The article we read helped me understand how science is related to the rest of life. Isn't that important?"

Rachel: "Yeah, but employers don't care about that kind of thing. They want you to know how to do technical scientific work, and that's it."

At that point, other students jumped in to add their thoughts. Most of them shared Cathy's sense that learning history is important and useful for science students, but they found it hard to give reasons for *why* they felt this way.

After some debate, they came up with a few reasons and concluded that science by itself cannot say what is valuable. They agreed that people have to understand things in a broader context in order to judge whether anything, even science itself, is worthy of attention. Also, while Rachel's job-market concern rang true for most of the students, they all admitted that employability isn't an automatic good. As one of the students said, "Let's say you get a job in your field, but you end up hating it or having to do things you believe to be wrong." The paycheck is a secondary matter, he suggested. Something more should enter the picture, something that provides a sense of value in the work we do.

His classmates agreed. They judged this "something more" to be of great importance, particularly for science students who take lots of focused, technical courses that don't zoom out very often to capture the broad perspective of value and motivation. Some of them even suggested that a zoomed-out history of science course like ours should be *required* for science students at our college.

I should say that all of this happened at a Christian college. These students understood that the school's curriculum, in every academic discipline and major, was framed and directed by an overarching Christian commitment. They knew that talking about a broad context would open up questions about religious faith, spiritual reality, and their own relationships with God and others. In fact, as Cathy expressed in her opening comment, the students considered these to be urgent questions and were eager to think about them in connection with their academic work.

Here was a group of top-notch science students sailing through challenging technical programs and, in many cases, headed for graduate school to earn PhDs. And all of their scientific learning left them wanting something more. They wanted a college education that would give them more than scientific knowledge and skill. They wanted to think as Philippians 4:8 directs Christians to think: "Whatever is true, whatever is noble, whatever is right, whatever is pure, whatever is lovely, whatever is admirable—if anything is excellent or praiseworthy—think about such things." Of course, what they had learned in their science courses remained dear to them, but they hoped to understand how all of that mattered in light of their commitments and value judgments.

Reading Changes Things

But why did the students get so riled up at that early hour? What was so jarring about the article they had read? All it did was trace the history of two familiar terms, *religion* and *science*. How could that be so unsettling? Remember that these were *Christian* students majoring in *scientific* fields like biochemistry, physics, and geology. They regarded science and religion as familiar categories. They were confident that scientists could live faithful lives and that Christians could have faithful motivations for pursuing scientific careers. But now the assigned article raised questions of a surprising sort. Without claiming that science and religion are incompatible, it showed that both categories are more complicated than most people assume.[1]

The article helped students see that the modern idea of science is an invented idea. Today we rely on experts—scientists—to "do" science and to tell the rest of us about their scientific conclusions. But consider this: the term *scientist* didn't appear until the 1800s! Before that, who was in charge of saying what science is, how it is to be done, or what its implications are? The surprising answer is *no one*, because our familiar idea of science had not yet emerged. Or maybe we should say that many people—philosophers, theologians, historians, mathematicians, and physicians—were in the process of *creating* science and establishing scientific institutions with social standing and political power. Our modern idea of science took root only about two hundred years ago, when it was cultivated by professional societies, government agencies, and university programs. My students found it disturbing to see that their beloved "hard sciences" could be so soft as to depend on cultural history and societal dynamics.

According to this same article, the meaning of "religion" has also changed over time. Before 1600 this term usually referred to the loving, personal commitment that tied the human heart to God. Nowadays we often speak of religion as a set of beliefs, as if it can be reduced to a list of propositions that people can accept or reject on an intellectual basis. To put it another way, religion now seems to be seated more in the head than in the heart, just the reverse of how it used to be.

Why did this shift occur? My students were surprised to read that it was part of a greater cultural trend connected with the Age of Enlightenment. During the seventeenth century, people started trying as never before to base their decisions and judgments on empirical evidence. This kind of thinking would eventually allow science to mature, but it would also have immediate social consequences. For instance, England was the site of heated political struggles involving several different groups that claimed to possess the unadulterated Christian revelation. In sorting out the competing claims, the British government relied heavily on advice from the newly formed Royal Society, which was devoted to "experimental learning" and was to become one of the world's most influential scientific institutions. Consequently, evidence-based thinking made its way into the political decision-making process. Governmental authorities decided that truth claims had to be tested on the basis of publicly accessible knowledge. In matters of faith, claims of personal revelations would not do. "True religion" had to produce claims that could be tested against established biblical doctrines and observable realities in the material world.

Can you see why this reading assignment threw my students for a loop? Suddenly the categories of science and religion could not be separated cleanly. The idea of science was now rooted in a history of philosophical and political wrangling over religion. And the idea of religion was now colored by an emphasis on evidence and empirical reasoning. Seeing the interdependence of categories led the students to doubt their usual ways of talking about issues of science and faith.

To call this a jarring experience would be an understatement. As science majors, the students were accustomed to looking *through* the lenses of chemistry, physics, and calculus. Now they were using different lenses—historical, philosophical, and theological lenses—to look *at* their scientific disciplines. From this perspective, science proved to have an unfamiliar shape and texture. It turned out that there was a whole new dimension to the world that the students had come to know and love so well. A new world of history and culture lay behind their familiar world of molecules and tectonic plates. Discovering this world behind the world was both unsettling and thrilling. It was like a conversion experience. Reading about history had transformed their understanding of science.

Seeing the World Anew

The students had had what might be called an "existential moment," when realities that you usually ignore suddenly strike you as deeply important. At moments like this you see the world anew and are forced to see yourself in a new role. In that world behind the world, you may have additional responsibilities and a heightened sense of calling. You enter a new kind of existence, and you have to reorient yourself to an altered field of possibilities.

My students still wanted to become scientists, but now they saw that this would require more discernment and skill than they had anticipated—at least, that is, if they wanted to be completely true to their Christian calling. The surprising breadth of that calling was the first lesson they learned in our course. Prior to our readings and discussions, they had not understood how science is fundamentally connected to philosophy, to religion, and to cultural attitudes. But once they saw this, they knew there was work to do, and they wanted to understand more about the connections. They wanted to develop the kind of mental agility that would allow them to move within and beyond science in effective ways. And this is why they decided that history of science courses like ours were so important. These courses could provide them with important training for the task ahead.

That decision served the students well. By studying history, they learned things about science that science courses do not teach. By stepping outside of science, they deepened their understanding of what science is. The broader context allowed them to see how value judgments and human commitments operate within science and give it cultural authority. In colleges and universities today, the experts who best understand value-laden contexts usually reside in humanities departments specializing in history, philosophy, literature, and language. My students gained a new appreciation for the importance and usefulness of learning from scholars and teachers in these areas. Humanities-style reflection led these students through key existential moments and helped them find their bearings in the world they were discovering.

So Much More

Many Christian students crave this kind of education, believing that the truth of Christ can shine in the most surprising places and produce transformed visions of a fallen world. They also believe that they are called to live in accordance with this truth, and they want to respond faithfully to that calling. This is why a Christian college education should not only provide training for the job market but also train students—even science students—to recognize the pervasive reality of grace and to discern the gospel's radical implications for their lives and careers. Discernment of this sort requires cultural knowledge, value judgments, and a framework for assessing the most basic of human commitments. It should be no surprise, then, that the humanities have such importance in the Christian college curriculum.

But let's admit that Christian education depends on more than good courses and knowledgeable, caring teachers. Students also have to play an active role. They have to open their eyes if they are going to see the world anew. They have to buckle down and study if they want a full return on the tuition dollars they have invested. The temptation to take an easier road will always be there. I have seen a number of students yield to this temptation because they thought their families and churches had taught them all they need to know about faith. Students with this mind-set want only the skills and credentials that will help them secure a comfortable financial future for themselves. They aspire to get good at science, for instance, but they don't want their motivations, worldviews, and life plans to be challenged in any way. For them, education is not about investing in faith and helping it grow and mature; it is about keeping faith safe and secure, like a buried treasure.

I hold out hope that students like this will recognize that so much more is being offered to them—so much more that can contribute to a faithful renewing of their minds.

With the renewing of a mind comes the sharpening of a conscience. As my students reconsidered the categories of science and religion, they embarked on more than an academic exercise. Besides learning to understand these categories in a new way, they also developed the habit of *looking for* and *correcting* the distortions that had been created by their old ways of understanding. For instance, they started noticing and criticizing the conflicting messages that are used to promote science to different people. In the halls of government, there is an emphasis on science as a key to economic and military strength. If educational institutions want to receive federal money that supports those goals, they have to attract students into the sciences. But the messages that colleges send to potential science students are usually filled with promises of creative freedom, intellectual satisfaction, and the thrilling quest for foundational truth. So what is the point of science? National security? Attracting grants and students? The joy of learning? The answer depends on where you sit. Science is not one, monolithic thing that has a single purpose, and not everyone values it for the same reasons. Once my students saw how science can be seen from different angles, they started to examine their own value judgments and motivations for pursuing science. Spurred by a desire to be truthful and honest, they became humbly reflective and open to correction.

If students take a historical, zoomed-out view of science, they will surely see that science paves the way to technological advancement, sophisticated workplaces, increased wealth, devastating weaponry, and fast-paced, high-stress patterns of life. With the good comes the bad. While some problems are solved, others are created. And for this reason, reflective students will have to think about their own culpability. They enter science knowing that they will be expected to comply with the norms and expectations of governmental or educational institutions. Will they make peace with institutional frameworks in order to gain comfort, respect, authority, or financial security? Will this kind of compliance comport with their moral or religious sense of responsibility? Or will their happiness and scientific accomplishments come at the expense of their concerns for justice, mercy, and humility? These are vexing questions that students will face not only in college but also at various stages of their professional lives.

The relevance of these questions underscores the importance of history and other humanities courses in a Christian college education. It is the job of such courses to give students a broad view of human experience and to help them prepare for the inevitable existential moments in their lives. Students in humanities courses reflect on the dreadful reality of suffering and injustice in the world and also on examples of redemption in specific human contexts. In the long term, the wisdom and virtue instilled by this kind of education can help students stay mindful of their values and callings. Anyone concerned with the career-long challenge of trying to "do the right thing" in every circumstance would do well to cultivate good habits of reflection and discernment. And for this reason, studying the humanities is important for all Christian college students, no matter which subjects they choose to major in.

Notes

1. Peter Harrison, "'Science' and 'Religion': Constructing the Boundaries," *The Journal of Religion* 86 (2006): 81–106.

Ruining the Movies?

Carl Plantinga, Film and Media Studies

Movies are a pervasive and important presence in our lives. Movies may have provided some of the most powerful emotional experiences we have had. Characters like Batman, Shrek, and Frodo Baggins are as familiar as friends. The joyous memories of watching the latest Hollywood release with family and peers are a testimony to the emotional power that media have.

But why should anyone *study* the movies? Movies are for escape, aren't they? Movies are portals into fantastic and imaginative worlds. Movies present stories that excite and thrill us or perhaps fulfill some kind of therapeutic function, dealing with our fears and assuring us that everything will be okay. Movies show us that good and evil are easily distinguishable, that good always wins, that we are all on the road to moral perfection, and that we will make the right choices in the end. When we *study* the movies, on the other hand, we don't so easily accept their attractions. Instead, we question and analyze them. We learn how they function, how they tell stories and create characters and form fictional worlds—how they move us and make meaning. Why compromise the good feelings by peering at movies through the analyst's microscope? Why spoil the fun? Why ruin the movies?

Careers and Vocation

Could studying the movies be *useful*? One way to answer this question is to talk about careers and vocation. A few years ago the *New York Times* ran an article with the title "Is a Cinema Studies Degree the New M.B.A.?" The background assumption was that the master of business administration was the all-purpose degree that maximized the graduate's employment opportunities. But the article points out the growing practical importance of film studies in higher education. The author notes that many cinema studies majors see their degree not necessarily as a calling card into the film and television industry, but rather as an immersion in "the professional language of the future." The language of movies, which we might call "multimedia communication," is not merely a visual language. Multimedia communication is broad and eclectic, a combination of written and spoken language, moving and still photographs, sound and music. It draws together the skills of writing and storytelling, cinematography and photography, sound recording, music making, and the digital manipulation of graphics and images.

Multimedia communication is pervasive. We see it not just on the big screens of the movie theaters but also on the small screens of televisions, computers, and even phones. Multimedia communication is also powerful. It is a favored mode of persuasion for politicians, advertisers, nonprofit organizations, and the government. And multimedia communication is versatile. It conveys fiction, advertising, and the news of the day.

Every educated person should learn the multimedia equivalents of "reading" and "writing." Media literacy is now a standard skill for careers and vocations as diverse as law, politics, business, the military, advertising, public relations, and the media industries. Film and media majors become well-versed in both making and understanding the media; they become experts in multimedia literacy. Those with a strong interest in creative media-making learn to use cameras to make stunning images, both moving and still. They learn to record music and sound. They learn about graphics and voice-over narration. They learn how to put it all together into a clear and compelling multimedia presentation. And all film and media majors also learn to write in the conventional sense. They write not only screenplays and teleplays but also critical and analytical papers—the kinds of analyses you'll see in all types of writing, from film reviews to scholarly books. A film and media major prepares them for a wide range of careers.

Movies and the Humanities

Could studying the movies *build character*? This question gets at the place of film and media studies in the context of an education in the humanities. A humanities education isn't just about careers; it is also aimed at the whole person—at personal growth, fulfillment, and identity. The original question—Why ruin the movies?—is a species of a broader question: Why "ruin" anything at all by understanding it better? Certainly, we can see the direct benefits of "instrumental" knowledge. To make a brilliant video, a student needs to learn how to use cameras, lights, and editing software. But what about knowledge with less-obvious benefits? Should we study the movies as part of an overall well-rounded education? And what education do we need in order to appreciate, for example, James Cameron's blockbuster films *Titanic* or *Avatar*? The answer to these questions depends on what we mean by "appreciate."

A humanities education is largely about making connections. We understand the world around us more deeply when we see how one thing is connected to another, when we see how interconnected everything really is. It is all good and fine to be able to perform concrete tasks well, but we gain something invaluable by learning to understand the world at the deep level of conceptual connections, to anticipate the consequences implied by certain decisions, and to make creative decisions based on the range of possibilities and outcomes we see. This deeper understanding separates the technicians from the visionaries.

I often give my students two reasons to study film. There are no doubt other reasons, but these are the two I embrace. The first is that the cinema is a great art form, and the arts are a gift from God. We were given the arts in part to delight us, to contribute to the full lives we are meant to live. But they offer us more than just delight. Narrative artworks like films and novels present us with stories that can be both delightful and instructive. Sometimes we label movies as "art films" if they are beautiful, moving, insightful, challenging, and important in film history. These films are playgrounds for the imagination, providing opportunities for us to expand our horizons. They educate our emotions, even when we are unaware that they are doing so. This is to say that they have emotional power over us. As narratives, they show us the lives of fictional characters in all kinds of situations and depict a vast range of human experiences. In this way they help us put our own experiences in context. So studying art films can be a way of studying our own imaginations and emotions. It can help us know ourselves.

The second reason to study film is that like most of the popular arts, films reflect and reinforce the values and expectations of our culture. They therefore play a powerful role in shaping the individual lives we live out within our cultural context. Some have called our formation by popular culture "the other education." When we study film in this sense, we might pay just as much attention to blockbuster films such as *Avatar* and *Titanic* as we do to the art films of well-regarded directors like Joel and Ethan Coen or Hayao Miyazaki. The point here is not, as English poet Matthew Arnold put it, to study "the best that has been thought and said," but rather to consider what has had an impact on our culture. For in addition to teaching us about ourselves, films (especially popular films) can teach us about the people around us and the societal values that define our cultural landscape.

Making Connections: *Avatar* and *Titanic*

I can assume that most of my students will have seen *Avatar* and *Titanic* and that they will have found these films more or less fascinating. *Avatar* has grossed nearly 2.8 billion dollars in theatrical receipts, meaning that, at an estimated average of $8 per ticket, 345 million people have seen this film in movie theaters, and countless more have viewed it on DVD. More than two-thirds of the audience for *Avatar* comes from outside the United States. Hollywood doesn't make films for Americans anymore, but for an international audience. We tend to be intrigued by the new technologies of visual representation that director James Cameron employs in his films: 3-D, motion capture, and the compositing of live action and digital animation. What attracts people to Cameron's films is partly spectacle: the realistic portrayal of the sinking of the *Titanic*, or the beauty and exoticism of the alien world of Pandora in *Avatar*. And the stories themselves are intriguing, at least in some ways. *Avatar* tells the story of Jake, an ex-marine who fights as a mercenary for a corporation that invades the world of an alien species, the Na'vi. After falling in love with a Na'vi princess, Jake helps defend her people against the invasion and ultimately gives up his human identity to become a Na'vi himself.

But to appreciate *Avatar* in a deep sense, one must be able to make connections. Cameron's visualization of the flora and fauna of Pandora, for example, can be traced back to diverse sources, from Walt Disney to art nouveau, from science fiction illustrator Roger Dean to Leonardo da Vinci (for the design of marvelous little "helicopter creatures"). Like most movies that attain the status of "an event," the sources for and implications of the story of *Avatar* have been endlessly examined on the Internet. Whereas in high art, literary allusions and visual "quotations" are celebrated for their conscious references to other works of art (what some critics call "intermediality"), commercial works such as *Avatar* are much more likely to receive criticism, perhaps unfairly, for calculated manipulation and lack of originality. Thus many have pointed out the similarities of *Avatar* to other stories that feature the meeting of two very different cultures and a romance that implies both the possibility and the difficulty of unity and peace between the two cultures. *Pocahontas* and *Dances with Wolves* immediately come to mind, but the sources go back much further. Another convention in *Avatar* is the extended concluding battle; this is a standard element in many Hollywood blockbusters, including all of the superhero films and even the more respected *Lord of the Rings* trilogy. (The implication of "redemption through violence" is especially ironic in a film such as *Avatar* that preaches peace but ends with dozens of minutes of cathartic fighting.) One can also compare the story of *Avatar* with recent political and cultural struggles, most obviously the Indian wars, Vietnam, and perhaps Iraq. Some critics have seen the film as anti-military and anti-American, while others have claimed that the film takes a stand against "corporate colonialism." Cameron's story is also firmly environmentalist, and in representing the Na'vi as living in harmony with nature, it obviously draws from Romantic conceptions of native peoples as harboring deep wisdom about the natural world and how to live in it. To learn about these kinds of connections is to appreciate *Avatar*, not in the sense of "liking" it but rather in the sense of understanding the sources of its ideas and the influence it may have as a mass narrative in the imaginations of millions.

James Cameron may be the most calculating and crafty filmmaker working today, in that he knows how to fashion a story that appeals to mass audiences. One essential aspect of his most popular films goes less noticed by critics: his understanding of the audience's need or desire for transcendence. In *Avatar*, one sees this in the pantheistic religion of the Na'vi, who communicate with the goddess Eywa by making intimate contact with nature, for instance by literally connecting their hair braids to various flora and fauna. One also sees the need for transcendence in Jake's deep desire to escape his very humanity and become something "better" than human. Motivated in part by his own damaged body, by his love for Princess Neytiri, and also by the inescapable sense that the Na'vi are somehow purer or closer to nature than human beings, Jake decides to become a Na'vi himself.

Cameron's recognition of our need for transcendence is even more pronounced in *Titanic*, in which Rose (Kate Winslett), speaking of her lover Jack (Leonardo DiCaprio), says, "He saved me in every way possible." In a fanciful scene at the end of the movie, we see Rose going to meet all the deceased victims of the long-sunk Titanic, who have now come back to life. Is this Rose's fantasy, a dream, or a vision of the afterlife? The old Rose has become young and beautiful once again. We see her as she enters the ship's architectural centerpiece, the Great Staircase, gleaming, miraculously new, brilliantly lit. There Jack, who long ago was lost in the North Atlantic, waits for her atop the staircase, and as all of the onlookers applaud, he takes her hand and they kiss as the camera tilts upward and moves toward a brilliant light. Fade to white.

Audiences can interpret this scene in many ways, but it clearly communicates the hope or belief that love will transcend death. In *Titanic*, the relationship of Jack and Rose embodies a vision of love and bliss that is an idealized and sentimental treatment of romantic love. For many audiences, this affirmation of the existence of love beyond death is a central element of the film's appeal. It is the salve that makes the wounds of death and grief bearable.

While *Titanic* may be a myth of eternal love, its portrayal of that love is open to multiple interpretations that connect in different ways with the various beliefs and desires of individual viewers. What could it mean for Jack to save Rose "in every possible way"? That seems like a tall order for romantic love. Most Christians would say that the ultimate saving love stems from another source—a loving God. But this is not to say that Christians should "see through" the romance in *Titanic* and interpret it as divine love. It may be more useful for Christians viewing this film to dwell on the dynamics of memory and hope in the face of tragedy. Understanding these universal elements of human experience is important if one wants to be empathetic and loving to one's neighbors.

To truly appreciate either *Titanic* or *Avatar*, to understand their roles in our culture, one needs to make connections. Making connections, in part, means being able to identify the worldviews of popular narratives and to understand the kinds of emotional and persuasive appeals that allow such narratives to resonate with so many people. This is the kind of wisdom that can be imparted through the film studies and other disciplines in the humanities.

Studying film and media can certainly lead to diverse careers, but it also contributes to a strong humanities education. In my teaching, I pay attention to great films and to not-so-great films. Sometimes the so-so films are especially intriguing for what they reveal about us as human beings— our worldviews and our deepest needs, desires, and beliefs. Making these sorts of connections is what a humanities education is all about.

Does this kind of analysis ruin the movies? Perhaps for some, but not for those who genuinely want to be educated, not for those who desire to make connections.

Why Stories Matter More Than Ever

A Letter to a Friend Just Beginning College

Jennifer Holberg, Literature

My dear C——,

I know I will sound like an old fogey (and I suppose I am, so thanks for your patience and good humor, as ever), but I cannot believe that you will soon be coming to college. What a deep delight it has been watching you grow into the wonderful person you are today—one for whom I have had such fond hopes ever since you were born (and even before, if truth be told). I am confident that these next years will be filled with rich ideas and amazing experiences as you continue to develop the many gifts God has given you. I'm excited by all the possibilities that lie before you!

When we talked the other day, I thought you raised some fine questions about our curriculum here at the college. I know you're eager to choose a major (or rather, decide which of the seven or so in which you're currently interested is the one you are going to pursue!), and to be honest, you have a number of fine choices. But maybe it will help narrow your decision if I, as your friend and honorary aunt, can give you some insight into my own discipline: English literature.

When you major in English (as you know I did, along with history), you often hear the question "What can you do with that when you graduate?" So before you begin this first year, it is worth it, I think, to ask yourself what learning itself is for. Why are you in college? Increasingly, some folks seem to think that you are coming to college to acquire as much data as you can stuff in your brain before you go off to your post-college job. For these people, education is simply content delivery:

You come to class.

The professor gives you information.

You process it and give it back in the form of a test, paper, or lab report.

The professor grades you.

The end.

In the English classroom, this often means that I have some students who come into my class worried because literature doesn't seem to have easily defined "stuff." There seems to be lots of discussion where the professor constantly asks students how *they* understand the texts before them. Worse, literature seems like a secret (and often frustrating) world of "hidden meanings," unconnected to the real world. Without the magic decoder ring of interpretation (that they are sure others must possess), these students don't know if the flower in the poem means love or death or sex. Or maybe it's just a flower? Ack!

And if that's exasperating for them, these same folks cannot see much connection between reading literature and preparing for a career (which is what they think college is truly about—getting a job). Of course, with the economy in its current shape, I'm not denying that you should have an eye to developing skills that will transfer into the world of work. But I believe learning to read deeply, to write compellingly, to research thoroughly, and to think critically—the skill set of the English major—has real connection to the multiple callings English majors pursue. In fact, our department has just redesigned its entire curriculum to help students think vocationally throughout their entire time in college, and has even taken the rather unusual step of requiring an internship for all of our majors. But I also believe it's shortsighted to see college as only data gathering and job preparation. You're probably familiar with the statistic that folks will switch jobs something like seven times during their lives—and end up working in environments vastly different from the ones in which they began. The way I studied in college looks a lot different from the way I teach my students today (with e-mail, readings on the web, responses online). From experience, we both know how rapidly all things technological change. I've told you before about the computer-programmer-in-training whom I dated as an undergrad; for his degree, he learned to code in computer languages that no one even thinks about today. So learning can't be only about the direct connection between course content and the exact application of that content to a job.

No, the question really becomes this: What skills, broadly defined, do you need to spend your college years honing? Put it another way: What habits of heart and mind will see you through a lifetime?

One of the most important of these habits is learning to be attentive. I love how one of my favorite contemporary writers, Marilynne Robinson, helps us focus on the object of this attentiveness:

> So I have spent my life watching, not to see beyond
> the world, merely to see, great mystery, what is
> plainly before my eyes. I think the concept of tran-
> scendence is based on a misreading of creation.
> With all respect to heaven, the scene of miracle is
> here, among us.

For me, studying literature is one key way to indeed behold that "scene of miracle."

But being attentive has always been difficult. Too often we miss the miracle. John Calvin (much like Robinson, who, by the way, often champions him today) emphasizes too that "sparks of God's glory" are everywhere: "You cannot in one glance survey this most vast and beautiful system of the universe, in its wide expanse, without being completely overwhelmed by the boundless force of its brightness." And yet, Calvin concludes, "certainly however much the glory of God shines forth, scarcely one man in a hundred is a true spectator of it." One in a hundred—those aren't great odds. Calvin's sixteenth-century Geneva no doubt had its own kinds of interruptions; for us, our difficulty is being bombarded with information every millisecond, the con-stant competition for our consideration. You've read a good ways into this letter by now; in that amount of time, have you been tempted to stop to check your e-mail, respond to a text message, look in at Facebook, fiddle with your iPod? If not, you are more disciplined than I am. Even as I've been writing this, the steady pinging of my e-mail has been a consistent call to stop writing, to stop attending to what I am doing: read this, click here, download that. T. S. Eliot in *The Four Quartets* diagnosed us all well when he said that we are "distracted from distraction by distraction." We flit from one thing to the next, never focusing on anything in a deep or sustained way. So often our knowledge is all surface, no depth.

So how does studying literature—either for a core literature requirement or even more for students who major in it—help us move, intellectually, into the deep end of the pool? I know you've heard some explanations: that literature is important because of its aesthetic qualities, the different kinds of beauty that it presents to us and helps us learn to appreciate; that literature is important because it provides insight into culture and history and ways of thinking different from our own; that literature is important because it shows us language at play.

Certainly, all of these are true, but I think the most compelling reason to study literature today is because stories have become the fundamental way our culture processes information. In other words, it's a primary way for us to pay attention—or rather, to call attention—to what we think is important. The going currency these days is not facts but narrative. In fact, I believe we are story-shaped people. Since the nineteenth-century (and undoubtedly before), we've been told of the power of the imagination, how poets, storytellers, people who control the imagination are the "unacknowledged legislators of the world." We all use stories to imagine the possibilities life may offer us. Do you remember all the times I came over to hang out with your mom and dad as you were growing up? At five and ten and fifteen years old (though it changed over time), you were constantly telling me about what you were going to do when you grew up, what job you would have, where you might travel, what your wedding would look like, how many children you would have. Right now, I'd wager, you could tell me a story about what you think this next year will bring. We know the reverse is true as well: we can probably both think of people whose lives get stuck because they can't imagine a different narrative possibility for their lives, can't imagine living out a different story line.

Through stories, we come to understand the expectations and norms of others around us—our family, community, church, and larger culture. Indeed, right or wrong, stories define those expectations and norms—and tell us whether we should think our lives are successful or not. Think about your high school experience: In the school assembly you had on drunk driving, did the principal discuss the legal penalties for drunk driving in order to persuade your fellow students, or did someone (perhaps a mom or dad) present the story of a life taken too soon? Or think about many of the moral issues of our times: Have people's attitudes changed because the laws have changed? Or have the laws changed because of the growing number and popularity of stories that presented a world where it seemed necessary for the laws to alter? Narrative has assumed an importance that makes it vital that we understand how stories work, and also which ones are life affirming and which are not. Stories both encourage and constrain us, depending on our own ability to critically interpret and respond to these narratives—and to write new ones.

As Christians, you and I understand this. After all, we know about the incredible power of story, even if we haven't always acted like it, because we have "the greatest story ever told." In his book *Who's Afraid of Postmodernism*, my friend, the philosopher Jamie Smith, reminds us that "too many Christians have bought into the modernist valorization of scientific facts and end up reducing Christianity to just another collection of propositions. . . . But isn't it curious that God's revelation to humanity is given not as a collection of propositions or facts but rather within a narrative—a grand sweeping story from Genesis to Revelation?" How often we forget this amazing notion: the Bible is not primarily a list of rules and regulations, but an astonishing *true* story about a God who loves humanity and wants to redeem it.

What's even more wonderful is that this "grand sweeping story" is one that includes us. We have the incredible privilege not only to live in God's world, but to be an active part of God's story. I like how Barbara Brown Taylor puts it: "Our lives are God's sign language to a sin-sick world, and God has promised us the grace we need to point the way home." Think about that: we are God's sign language! All that we do and say are the "words" that help to tell the story of the Word Made Flesh. The more we know, then, about God's world through narrative (both the biblical narrative and literature itself) the more we can find ways of more fully knowing not only each other but God, the "author and finisher of our faith."

In fact, Henry Zylstra, who taught in Calvin College's English department in the middle of the 20th century, argued that literature gives us "more to be Christian with." In other words, reading literature should help us fulfill our highest calling of loving God and loving our neighbors. That doesn't mean, of course, that everything we read must be Christian somehow or, worse, that we must "Christianize" it. Instead it means that the study of literature has a fundamentally moral dimension to it—moral in the sense that every text has an underlying perspective on the nature of the world, what it sees as truth, what it defines as the good. As part of the Harry Potter generation, you probably aren't surprised by this assertion. After all, what are the Harry Potter books but an extended meditation on the struggle between good and evil and on the ideal of self-sacrificial love?

Even so, I don't want you to think that I am advocating that we only read texts that are ultimately happy or "redemptive" or from which we can wring an easy lesson. Not at all. That would, quite simply, be shielding ourselves from the brokenness of our world—and that's no way to love God or neighbor. Actually, we don't want easy stories either way: unrealistically cheerful or unremittingly bleak. Both encourage us to embrace cliché over reality. That's not good life or good literature. Katherine Paterson, an award-winning children's author—but whose works have also been banned and sometimes criticized—argues: "As I write, I cannot tiptoe about trying not to step on the toes of nice people. I have to write as truly as I can about our human experience because if I falsify that experience, how can children find hope and encouragement in what I say?" Similarly, in her novel *Adam Bede*, the nineteenth-century British writer George Eliot nicely ridicules readers who only want characters to act in a predictable fashion:

> Let your most faulty characters always be on the wrong side, and your virtuous ones on the right. Then we shall see at a glance whom we are to condemn, and whom we are to approve. Then we shall be able to admire, without the slightest disturbance of our prepossessions: we shall hate and despise with that true ruminant relish which belongs to undoubting confidence.

Don't you love that phrase, "ruminant relish"? Eliot wants us to picture here a reader who is like a cow chewing its cud—mindless and placid and rather smug. Instead, Eliot wants us to *ruminate*—to think deeply—and examine our presuppositions, to understand the complexity of human experience, to know that the hero won't be wearing a white hat. Literature can only give us "more to be Christian with" if, as Paterson and Eliot suggest, it is fully grounded in all the splendor and squalor that we know is our essential condition.

Why is this so important? Why is reading about all kinds of people in all kinds of situations a good investment of four years of your time and talent? To add to your faithfulness in paying attention. I want you to be someone who notices the significant things in life and responds to them with the charity required by our faith. Honestly, though, living attentively with charity and empathy is difficult—something that we need daily work at becoming even a little better at. So, let me leave you with an example from my classroom of one thing I try with my students.

There's a long tradition in English of poems that comment on other forms of art, called ekphrastic poetry. On the first day of class, then, I begin class with a painting attributed to Bruegel projected on the screen at the front of the room. In the painting's foreground, a man and his horse are plowing a field; in the middle section, a man is tending sheep, and ships are sailing along; in the background are mountains and a city. All in all, a bustle of human activity, everyone absorbed in the business of living.

Except the painting has one more element: if you look very carefully in the bottom right-hand corner—near the shepherd on land and largest of the sailing ships at sea—you will see a pair of legs upended out of the sea. Almost none of my students ever spot this pair of legs—why should they, with so much else going on in the painting? And yet, the painting is entitled *The Fall of Icarus*. You remember the story of Icarus, I know: He and his father, Daedalus, escape from their imprisonment by making wings out of feathers and wax. Although Icarus is warned to not fly too close to the sun, lest it melt his wings, he becomes so excited by the feeling of flying that he rises higher and higher until, of course, his wings melt, he falls, and he is drowned in the sea.

In Bruegel's representation, however, this dramatic and tragic story makes no impact on the witnesses, because none of them seem to notice that it is happening—or even worse, if they do notice, they don't act on what they see. Now, you would think that seeing a boy with wings falling from the sky might generate some reaction, but Bruegel's people are all looking somewhere else, caught up in their own practicalities.

One possible way of reading this painting is through using the lens of literature. In his ekphrastic poem "Musée des Beaux Arts," W. H. Auden reflects on the people's lack of reaction in the painting, observing:

> In Breughel's Icarus, for instance: how everything turns away
> Quite leisurely from the disaster; the ploughman may
> Have heard the splash, the forsaken cry,
> But for him it was not an important failure; the sun shone
> As it had to on the white legs disappearing into the green
> Water; and the expensive delicate ship that must have seen
> Something amazing, a boy falling out of the sky,
> Had somewhere to get to and sailed calmly on.

In a way, this painting—especially when refracted through the lens of Auden's poem—reminds me a little bit of the story of the good Samaritan, where the first two men that pass by the wounded man are not moved by the "important failure" that they see. Their busyness blinds them, and they don't act as their faith would have them.

Pieter Bruegel the Elder (?). *The Fall of Icarus.* c. 1555–56. Oil on panel transferred to canvas, 29 × 44⅛ in. Musée d'Art Ancien, Musées Royaux des Beaux-Arts de Belgique, Brussels. With permission of Scala/Art Resource, New York.

We can relate, I know—we are all busy, we all have "somewhere to get to," and so, boys drown all around us, metaphorically, every day. Not only does literature show us the great need of the world and remind us of our responsibility to pay attention, but literature also calls us to respond to the world's needs and to live out our part in God's story of redemption. My hope is that you will never be someone who merely witnesses "something amazing" and then "sails calmly on" in the face of calamity. May the literature that you read make you ever more attuned to the stories of brokenness and blessing all around you.

Keep in touch, and tell me how your first semester goes. I'm eager to hear your stories!

Every blessing,
Jennifer

P.S. If you want to read more, here are some of the people to whom I referred:

- Marilynne Robinson, from "Psalm 8" in *The Death of Adam*
- John Calvin, from Book One of the *Institutes of the Christian Religion*
- Barbara Brown Taylor, *Speaking of Sin*
- Henry Zylstra, *Testament of Vision*
- Katherine Paterson, "Image and Imagination," in *Shouts and Whispers: Twenty-One Writers Speak about Their Writing and Their Faith*
- George Eliot, *Adam Bede*

Why Come to College to Study Writing?

Gary Schmidt, Writing

At the end of August 1837, Ralph Waldo Emerson rode into Cambridge from his home in Concord, to deliver an address to the Phi Beta Kappa Society as part of the graduation ceremonies of Harvard University. A year before, he had published "Nature," his most radical essay, and the members of the Society were eager to hear what he had come up with now—perhaps something equally countercultural. They filled the lecture hall, crowded the aisles, stood in the breathless back, and leaned in through the open windows as he began.

They were not disappointed: Emerson's lecture, "The American Scholar," became what one writer called America's "intellectual declaration of independence." No longer should American writers be dependent upon "foreign harvests," Emerson cried. Americans should develop their own writing, their own styles, their own topics, their own literary traditions. "Events, actions arise, that must be sung, that will sing themselves."

Probably in the hall was the student David Henry Thoreau, who had graduated the previous day and was eager for what was to come into his life. Whether he listened to

Emerson or read the lecture later, Thoreau felt that Emerson's oration suggested whole new possibilities. "He brought my blood to a boil," Thoreau wrote. Six weeks later, Thoreau had changed the order of his first two names and begun keeping the journal that would eventually lead to the writing of *Walden*, a book that, as Thoreau noted in the first pages, is "particularly addressed to poor students." It would become one of the axles of the American Renaissance. And if you're going to be a writer in America, you should have a copy on your desk right now.

When Thoreau wrote that his blood was brought to a boil, he did not mean that he was enraged, as we might understand the phrase today. Nor did he mean that he was all riled up, as is the cheap and easy purpose of most of today's political commentators. He meant that he was filled with a new passion, a new understanding, a new sense of purpose. He felt that he must act. To put it shortly, he was saying that his experience with Emerson's words had changed him forever.

This is why you come to college to study the art of writing: because your words can change a reader forever. And if your words are to change a reader forever, you must learn the art and practice of the craft. And if your words are to change a reader forever, you must confront head-on the practical and impractical qualities of your vocation. And if your words are to change a reader forever, you must confront the ethical quandaries that your skills pose. And if you want to change a reader forever, then you had better think about writing well.

But perhaps we are moving too quickly here. First things first: What is your job as a writer?

The Job of a Writer

Certainly, your job as a writer is to write. But what do you write about? What forms do you choose to write in? What do you want to say when you write? To whom do you write? What effects do you hope for in those to whom you write? How do you achieve those effects? Are you responsible for those effects?

These questions I've just listed are just the start.

Perhaps predictably, classical writers were varied in their responses about the writer's vocation. What is the job of the writer? The Sophists of ancient Greece argued that the writer writes because he (and they assumed that all writers would be "he") has skill with language; his job is to weave persuasive arguments and wonderful tales by means of his lovely style. Plato rejected that claim and argued that the writer is a man of wisdom and understanding who is committed to truth; the job of the writer is to bring that truth to his reader. Aristotle argued that the writer is a man of good sense, virtue, goodwill, and proper experience; his job is to use all those qualities to create works of truth. Cicero combined some of these elements: he argued—perhaps unhelpfully—that the job of the writer is to be a good man who writes well.

Does something seem to be missing here?

Let's return for a moment to New England, but to a period earlier than that of Emerson and Thoreau, and to a place a few miles southeast of Concord. Here is the pilgrim William Bradford, beginning his story of the history of Plymouth Plantation and explaining to his readers (mostly the other settlers of Plymouth, since no one else read it during Bradford's lifetime—or for that matter for another two hundred years) what his purpose is in his writing—and we'll use his seventeenth-century spellings if for no other reason than Bradford would have wanted it so: "And first of ye occasion and inducements ther unto; the which that I may truly unfould, I must begine at ye very roote & rise of ye same. The which I shall endeavor to manifest in a plain stile, with singular regard unto ye simple trueth in all things, at least as near as my slender judgmente can attaine the same."

For William Bradford, the writer's job is this: To speak in a logical, ordered way. To use language that a reader can understand. To write the truth, recognizing (with some humility) that his judgments may not always be accurate. To serve his community with his writing—here, by telling the story of that community's foundations and purposes.

Plainness, truth, and service. Or, in Aristotle's terms, good sense, virtue, and goodwill in the service of telling a story to an audience.

This sounds right. But something still seems to be missing. Is this the entire job of the writer?

For most of us, what seems to be missing here might be expressed in this single word: *delight*.

In the twentieth century, the writer E. M. Forster captured this part of the writer's task in a series of lectures that he delivered at Cambridge University in the spring of 1927, at a time when there were some serious questions about the role of art in a country that had seen an entire generation of young men wiped out in the bloody trenches and fields of World War I. Speaking of fiction, Forster gave this surprisingly simple explanation for what a writer is to do: the novelist's most important job is—Are you ready for this?—to tell a story. It's not about the Sophists' lovely language, or Plato's apprehension of truth, or Aristotle's ethical man, or Cicero's good man writing well; it's about telling a story that grips the reader. A novel, Forster writes, "can have only one merit: that of making the audience want to know what happens next."

And here we sense something true, not only for novels, but for all writing. There must be something there that makes us want to know what comes next. The writer's job is to make the reader want to turn the page—whether that page is made of pulp or pixels.

Now, let's see if we can put all of these together.

If a book entitled *On Christian Doctrine* seems an unlikely place to think about delight, the author, St. Augustine, may have been prone to chide you for your shortsightedness. He argued that the writer is doing something very serious. The tools that the writer uses—words—are signs of real things, wrote Augustine, and that means that the writer is dealing with the real stuff of the real world. That matters, Augustine insisted. Words are important not because they are lovely and persuasive in their loveliness, but because they bring us to the reality that lies around us. The implication here is an important one, and daunting, he warned, for it is this: By using words, the writer is evoking reality, and in doing so, the writer is mirroring the creative act of God himself. The writer's incarnation of reality through language is a working-out of what it means to be created in God's image, who is the ultimate evoker of reality.

Or put it this way: Augustine is asking, have you wondered what it means to be created in the image of God? I mean, *really* wondered?

And now, the surprise—and the reason why Augustine might have smacked you for not thinking that he was writing about delight. If the writer uses the tool of words, then how does that tool work? Augustine's answer is this: through beauty. The beauty that lies within words and is evoked by words engages not just the Sophists' emotions and pleasure, not just Plato's sense of understanding truth, not just Aristotle's intellect—but the whole person. How does beauty do this? "It is difficult to say," Augustine equivocates. But as we can tell from our own experience, it is true nonetheless, he insists.

So—and here we are coming to that one thing that brings all of the other reasons for writing into unity—what is the writer's job? Augustine argues that the writer's job is to fear God, to seek his will, to be gentle in piety, to be knowledgeable about the world and the workings of language, and to be a reader—but above all of these, far far far above all of these, the writer is to love. Writing, he argues, is an act of love.

And so, should the writer be bringing knowledge into the world? he asks. Yes. Should the writer be bringing beauty into the world? Yes. Should the writer be bringing wisdom into the world? Yes. But because writing is an act of love, the first question about the act of writing is not about whether writing brings knowledge or beauty or wisdom into the world. The first question is the one that William Bradford asked: Does the writing serve the world?

The job of the writer is to serve. That service is done through bringing knowledge, beauty, even wisdom into the world—but writing is always, first, about serving.

Why should you come to college—most especially a college committed to a faith tradition—to study writing? You come to learn how to serve through your writing.

Sorry, that may not be what you wanted to hear. You may have wanted to hear that you come to college to learn to be the writer who becomes rich and famous, the literary toast of the town, the writer whose books appear in airport bookshops and on magazine bestseller lists and get made into movies by Stephen Spielberg and finally bring you onstage with David Letterman where you cross your legs and act suavely. Maybe you wanted to hear that the writer's job is to become famous. And who knows? Maybe some of those things will happen to you. The world is a strange and comic place. But to start with that desire is to start with the desire of a hack—and you don't need to go to college to learn to be a hack. *That* you can pick up on your own.

So, then, how does writing serve?

The Purposes of Writing

John Gardner begins his lovely, small book *On Moral Fiction* with a story drawn from Norse mythology. The story begins with the god Thor, who, having fashioned his powerful hammer, flies around the globe with it once a year to guard the world from the darkness, doom, and despair of the Ice Giants, who would destroy everything if they could. But great Odin sees that Thor is growing weary in this task, and the threat of the Ice Giants is looming. So he goes to the king of the Trolls and demands to know how he can keep the Ice Giants at bay. They fight, for the secret is a dear one, and finally Odin takes the troll king in a terrible armlock and demands the knowledge. Then king agrees, but he will only give it, he says, if Odin gives to him his all-seeing eye. Immediately Odin agrees; he plucks it out and hands it to the Troll king. "Now, tell me. How do we keep the Ice Giants at bay?" Odin hollers. So the king tells him: "You have to watch with both eyes."

Odin's might, Gardner claims, represents power and authority in the world, and it is maimed. Power and authority will not save the world from the Ice Giants, or from tyrannies, dictatorships, frauds, miscreants who have attained office, war, terrorism, hatred, princes and principalities, bigotry, deception, despair.

Thor's hammer represents art—art such as writing. We use art to hold back the Ice Giants through beauty, through understanding, through recognition, through vivid calls for justice, through vulnerability, through the powerful act of one soul speaking to another.

That is how the writer serves.

In the medieval world, many scribes ended their long and dull hand copying of a book with the words *ad usum*, meaning "for the use of," and then they named the audience that they thought would use the book. The book did not belong to the scribe, who had spent who knows how many hours laboriously copying in poor light and perhaps poorer temperatures. The book did not belong to those who supplied the parchment and ink. In some ways it did not even belong to the scriptorium that produced it. It belonged to the reader, for it was written in the reader's service.

It belonged to the reader, whose servant the writer was.

To be called to be a writer—to be called (*vocare*) into a vocation—is to be called into the service of the world through the gift of language. This is not about David Letterman; it is about something ever so much deeper. You, the writer, are *ad usum*.

Okay. Right about this time, you are getting ready to skip ahead, because there's a big question looming in the atmosphere above you, and the question you have is the same question that your parents have and your Aunt Helen has and Miss Saunders your high school English teacher has and your friend who is coming with you to college to study engineering has and perhaps the person who is one day hoping to marry you has. It's the same question that anyone who you told you'd like to be a writer has. It is this: Can I earn a living as a writer?

It is a fair question. If you are going to college and investing four years and more than a few bucks, it's reasonable to ask what this all leads to. After all, the gospel reminds us, workers are worthy of their hire.

The reason we have gone such a roundabout way to this moment in this essay is, I suppose, to lay the foundation for asking this question, because only by going through that somewhat purgatorial process do you get to ask it— and not be a hack. Why do you want to write? To say that you can't imagine doing anything else is no good; of course you can imagine doing lots of other things. To say that you want to be Lord Byron and express yourself while wearing a dark flowing cloak and standing on Welsh cliffs is no good, either; Byron has already done that, and you would only be a pale imitator. To say that you want to write because you want the world to take notice of you is as roundabout as this essay so far.

But to say that you want to write because you sense the gifts of the Lord in you, because you love the tools of the writer—words—because you take delight in those gifts and tools and because you think you might be able to use them in service and you want to know how—that gives you the right to ask the question without being a hack.

So, can you earn a living as a writer? Perhaps more specifically, you might ask this: How will coming to learn and grow in the craft at a college get me to the point where I can earn a living as a writer? Even more specifically, you might ask this: How will a faith-based college get me there?

Here is one answer: Yes, you can earn a living as a writer—but there are no guarantees. Of course, there are no guarantees that any major you choose will lead directly into the vocation you hope to enter, or that you will make a living at the vocation you chose as a freshman. Perhaps it would be nice if that were the way of the world, but let us say it aloud: it isn't. You go to college to learn, hoping to grow in wisdom and stature and knowledge and fear of the Lord, to encounter the many subjects and fields that the liberal arts offer, taking the opportunity to rub against those fields and to see if they warm you, and thus to become bigger, larger as a person—to have more to be a human being with.

But, will taking a major in writing lead to something real and solid?

Absolutely.

A major in writing should give you the ability to communicate ideas and concepts cogently and clearly—something that employers in law firms, social agencies, and magazine and newspaper houses are looking for.

A major in writing should give you the ability to understand and connect with an audience—something that employers in large and small retail businesses, publicity firms, and advocacy groups are looking for.

A major in writing should give you the ability to analyze and present comprehensively large bodies of facts and evidence—something that employers in all research-based professions, federal and state and local government agencies, and engineering and development firms are looking for.

A major in writing should give you the ability to persuade—something that all fund-raising, advertising, and recruiting agencies are looking for.

A major in writing should give you the opportunity to develop a love for and ability to handle language, something that employers in the publishing world, the entertainment business, and the academy are looking for.

A major in writing, in short, teaches the art of communication, of handling large bodies of evidence in useful and complete ways, of interpreting data that the writer can gear toward the needs of a reader, of using language to speak of the resources of one to the needs of the other. In that the craft of writing is all about helping one soul speak to another, it is vital in all fields—not simply the writerly fields that come to mind immediately: publishing, teaching, journalism.

And not to be shortchanged is the learning of the craft itself; one comes to college to learn to develop gifts that may be natural, but unformed or unexamined. Perhaps in this field more than in others, the writing instructor is a nurturer, taking the student's gifts and honing them and broadening them and helping the young writer see the possibilities that a skill in language brings.

Thus the gifted poet who has written free verse for so long may confront the bound form—the sonnet, the sestina, the ghazal—to see what a more restricted poetic shape might offer. The fiction writer may take a stab at a new genre and ask questions not only of content but of form: What is a braided narrative? How does it differ from the collage form? What are the advantages and most decided disadvantages of the flashback or flash-forward? How does a writer employ a limited third-person narrator? Or a multiple first-person narrator? How is dialogue manipulated so that it imitates but does not transcribe life? How are characters made round rather than flat? For the expository writer, how do a writer's warrants affect claims and the backing of those claims? How much leeway is allotted the memoirist in terms of re-creation? What are the boundaries of genres such as creative nonfiction, historical fantasy, steampunk?

College is the place where the writer, under instruction, encounters questions that will shape, guide, and affect his or her writing for an entire career. It is where you learn the craft among others learning their craft—your fellow students and your professors. And it is where you begin to imagine and develop—*really* imagine and develop—your own voice, your own style, your own ways of saying what you have to say.

Writing at a Faith-Based College

But why come to a faith-based college to do this? Here we come full circle. To answer that question we must begin with this: all writers want to affect their readers powerfully—either by engrossing a reader in a story, or moving a reader through drama, or surprising a reader with a line of poetry that makes him tip his hat, or changing a reader's perspective so that she sees an issue or an idea differently. Language is indeed powerful. And, as with any gift, that power needs and demands inspection and understanding. And writers need the equipment to do such inspection. Remember: being made in the image of God is not something to ever take lightly.

For if writing is to move people, change people, bring people to new awarenesses, then it is an ethical act—or at least an act that carries ethical motivations and responsibilities—and an act that mirrors, once again, God's creative image in us. A story—whether it is the story of the salvation of Israel or the story of green eggs and ham—is always told for a purpose. Thus writers need to be equipped with an awareness of the ethics of writing, and with an understanding of purpose, and with questions about their vocation that are spiritual in nature—beginning with the astonishing notion that God has revealed himself principally, orthodox Christians would argue, through narrative—a narrative that, in fact, teaches us those things which seem beyond all telling in all other modes.

So then, why write, if not to serve with what it is that you have to say? Why affect another, if not to elevate, to move, to encourage growth and awareness of each other as characters within God's largest narrative? If there is another answer, then let the writer see to it and examine whether that answer fits well with the whole of the writer's life, physical and spiritual.

For the writer who is a person of faith, here's why you write:

A year or so ago, I was leading a writing workshop for middle schoolers at a reservation school in northern Michigan. We worked on creating and building characters, and the students were terrific. They wrote with passion and imagination, and when I asked them to read what they had written aloud, most of the hands in the classroom went up.

But there was a kid in the back with a red shirt who hesitated, and who did not put his hand up. Through the hour I waited, and waited, and then, finally, he did put his hand up, and immediately I called on him to read his stuff. And he did, but his voice was so quiet that I could not hear it. So I said, "Tell me again," and immediately every eye in the room turned to him, and silence fell, and the kid in the red shirt put his hands in front of his face and would not speak.

We went on.

Later, I could see that he had written a lot, and I called on him again, since it seemed that he might be ready. But when the terrible eyes turned to him, he covered his face with his hands and would not speak.

After the workshop, the teacher called the class up to the front for snacks, and they went eagerly—except for the kid in the red shirt, who did not leave his seat. So I went back to him and said, "I think you have stories to tell, and I think you may have the gift to tell them." Well, he could not stop talking. He told me what he was writing, where he got his ideas, what he was reading, how the stories were about him and his cousin, and how one time . . .

And then one of his classmates came back with his snack, and sat down beside us, and the kid in the red shirt was done. He put his hands over his face, and was still.

So, do you want to be a writer? Come then, and see what it is all about. It is about learning the craft so that your skills are heightened and developed. But perhaps even more importantly, it is about learning that your purpose as a writer is to speak to the kid in the red shirt at the back of the class—no matter his age—so that you can say to him, I know it is a broken world. Fiction is always about a broken world. There is no denying that. But it is also a beautiful world, most worthy the winning. Poetry will never exhaust its praises, drama its complexities, nonfiction its wonders.

You write to serve the kid in the red shirt at the back of the room, to bring hope, light, order, companionship, reflection, recognition, understanding, beauty, humor, realism, expectation, guts.

You write so that the kid in the red shirt at the back of the room will see in your writing more than what he is, or has, or has experienced. You write to invite him to a larger world so that his hands will begin to come down from his face.

You write to bring his blood to a boil.

That's why you come to a faith-based college to major in writing.

Ad usum.

How a Speech Can Change an Audience

Why Studying Public Address Is Important

Kathi Groenendyk, Rhetorical Studies

On April 4, 1968, a white man shot and killed civil rights leader Martin Luther King Jr., and black communities across the country reacted in pain and anger. People rioted in 76 American cities, killing 46 people (most of them black) and injuring 2,500; police arrested 30,000 people.[1] Several white politicians blamed the black citizens—and even King himself—for the violence; blacks were angry and distrustful of all whites, especially since a single white man had killed their leader. In this volatile setting, presidential candidate Bobby Kennedy was scheduled to speak in an Indianapolis black neighborhood that night.

Kennedy's flight was late, and as the large, mostly black crowd gathered to hear him, news of King's assassination was spreading. Some in the audience began to shout insults at the whites nearest them; whites on the crowd's edge left in fear. Black militant gangs gathered support as the time passed, making violence more likely. With this crowd, the police were helpless. The local planning committee anxiously watched the mass of people, wondering whether Kennedy would be safe; they asked members of a nearby recreation center to check trees and windows for possible assassins.[2]

When Kennedy's airplane landed, his staff told him of King's death and the potential neighborhood violence. Despite the dangers, Kennedy drove to the neighborhood, writing notes for his speech on an envelope. He was going to have to speak extemporaneously—which was unusual for him—and he had only a general idea of what he wanted to say. When he arrived, the crowd was noisy; many in the front had not heard the news about King, so they were still cheering for Bobby. Kennedy stepped up to the microphone and announced, "Martin Luther King was shot and killed tonight." Many audibly gasped; several screamed. Shouts competed with Kennedy's next words: "Martin Luther King dedicated his life to love and to justice between fellow human beings. He died for the cause of that effort. In this difficult time for the United States, it is perhaps well to ask what kind of nation we are and what direction we want to move in."

It seemed that the crowd would erupt in anger and violence, yet Kennedy continued.

> We can move in that direction as a country in greater polarization, black amongst blacks and white amongst whites, filled with hatred toward one another; or we can make an effort as Martin Luther King did, to understand and to comprehend, and replace that violence, that stain and bloodshed that has spread across our land, with an effort to understand, compassion, and love. For those of you who are black and are tempted to be filled with hatred

and distrust of the injustice of such an act, against all white people, I can only say that I can also feel in my own heart the same kind of feeling. I had a member of my family killed, but he was killed by a white man.

Kennedy seemed emotional at this point, and the crowd began to quiet. Kennedy ended his speech:

My favorite poem, my favorite poet, was Aeschylus. He once wrote,

> even in our sleep, pain which cannot forget
> falls drop by drop upon the heart,
> until, in our own great despair,
> against our will,
> comes wisdom through the awful grace of God.

What we need in the United States is not division; what we need in the United States is not hatred; what we need in the United States is not violence and lawlessness, but is love, and wisdom, and compassion toward one another, and a feeling of justice toward those who still suffer within our country, whether they be white or whether they be black.

So I ask you tonight to return home, to say a prayer for the family of Martin Luther King . . . but more importantly to say a prayer for our own country, which all of us love—a prayer for understanding and that compassion of which I spoke.

The crowd quietly left. Through this speech, Kennedy took a crowd on the brink of violence and calmed them, recognizing their pain and offering them a different path for action.

When my students watch and listen to this speech in class, they hear the crowd's reaction and notice Kennedy's calm presence, the speech's rhythm, and his themes of peace and justice. Even though we are not Kennedy's intended audience, we are drawn into his speech. The students are quiet and intent; many say they feel a chill as Kennedy speaks and quiets the crowd. That, I tell my students, is a speech's potential: not just to persuade but to change an audience and its situation.

The Art of Rhetoric

The art of public speaking—rhetoric—is centuries old. It began in ancient Greece with the Sophists, Plato, and Aristotle, who defined rhetoric as the art of discerning in any given situation the available means of persuasion. Scholars during the Roman Empire further shaped rhetorical study and practice, emphasizing the need for speakers to uphold high ethical standards. Throughout the Renaissance and then again in the eighteenth century, rhetoric flourished. At various times, rhetoric was dismissed as merely empty, meaningless words used to manipulate, but most of rhetoric's history has emphasized a complex understanding of words, reasoning, audience adaptation, and awareness of situations. The best theorists minimized attention to mere delivery, focusing instead on the art of persuasion. Today, a quick review of the top 100 American speeches (which includes Kennedy's eulogy) reflects this complex rhetorical approach to public speaking: the great speakers have known how to choose content relevant to their audience and have shaped that content into a memorable message. Kennedy's speech is not successful because of his delivery; his speech is successful because it utilizes a variety of rhetorical strategies developed in this centuries-old study.

Despite rhetoric's great potential to bring change, most students do not want to take the basic public speaking class, nor do they see the value of studying the history of rhetoric or great public addresses. (When I was a graduate student at Penn State University, the public speaking requirement created so much anxiety that some students seriously considered dropping out of the university because of it.) Some students dread being in front of others. Some view a public speaking course as unnecessary. Then there are the few who enjoy performing and expect an easy A in the class simply on that basis. Yet, while it seems like almost no one takes rhetoric seriously early on, former students often tell me how important public speaking has become in their lives. The farmer who became an elder at church and had to speak at congregational meetings; the hairdresser who had to present her recent work to other stylists; the grade school teacher who had to talk to a room of parents and grandparents—none of these people were "born" public speakers, but they came to depend on the skill.

Effective communication is critically important for a variety of jobs. As indicated in countless surveys, strong communication skills are the number-one trait employers look for when hiring—not grade point average, major, or work experience. Intensive study of the discipline of rhetoric and public address (perhaps leading to a major or minor in this area) can prepare students for careers in ministry, law, public relations, journalism, teaching, and—of course—speech writing. Yet even a single public speaking class can help a student no matter his or her major or career goals. For example, I know an accounting major who recently took an argumentation class after an internship experience showed her that she needed to learn how to present information persuasively.

Learning Effective Speaking

An effective speaker considers the audience's interests and knowledge and crafts a speech around these. The crafting process involves careful research, development of a clear and engaging thesis, construction of logical arguments, stylistic attention to structure and language, and a delivery that impacts the audience. Of course, in the volatile situation of April 4, Bobby Kennedy had just a few moments to prepare, but his knowledge and training served him well under pressure. Students may feel pressures of their own when they have to speak, but having a reliable process for creating speeches can relieve some of the worries they have about their delivery skills.

A very shy and bright secondary education student enrolled in my speech class recently because she had been told by her professors that she needed to project more confidence when she spoke. She dreaded her speeches: she did not like looking at the audience, she didn't know what to do with her hands, and she spoke so quietly that her classmates could hardly hear most of her words. But once she learned that her grade would reflect not only her delivery but also her topic choice, her organization, and her use of language, she immersed herself in writing, researching, and outlining her speeches. By the time of her last speech of the semester, students in the class were eagerly listening for her poetic phrases and colorful analogies. Her careful crafting had made her a confident and engaging speaker.

Of course, a speech depends on more than poetically crafted phrases. Through the creative process of writing speeches, students also practice developing clear messages and solid arguments. At our college, at the end of every semester, the best speakers from each public speaking course participate in a departmental contest. The judges use criteria that weigh content, organization, and delivery. Occasionally, students who attend the contest question the choices of first-, second-, and third-place winners, pointing to problems with evidence or faulty analogies. I hope students will carry this kind of critical thinking with them into their other classes and into their lives as citizens. Cicero, the Roman statesman and rhetorical scholar, believed that a rhetorical education was necessary for an engaged and thoughtful political life; if students can evaluate a message's logic, they may be less likely to be swayed by mere charisma.

In her book *Eloquence in an Electronic Age*, communication scholar and news commentator Kathleen Hall Jamieson argues that in the past few decades rhetorical education has declined; students often do not take even one public speaking course.[3] As a result, students not only are missing a chance to practice an art that they will almost certainly be using in their own lives; they also are missing the chance to learn how to listen to and evaluate the speeches of others. Jamieson cautions us about the potential effects on our communities, our states, and our country: If listeners cannot judge the reasoning and rhetoric in a politician's speech, then they will have to rely on the spin of commentators. If we cannot independently evaluate the political arguments around us, how will we weigh our possibilities and choose particular ways of voting, participating in politics, and engaging with neighbors?

Students who do take a rhetoric class or a public address class gain important skills in learning to become an active part of a community. In a public speaking class, students become a part of an audience: They learn how to listen actively, to provide feedback, and to ask questions. They also learn how to sympathize with each other, because at the semester's start they all dread getting up in front of a group. In a public address class, students study great speeches, imagining themselves in the audience at that time and place. They develop their skills in identifying with others. On the one hand they consider what it must have been like to be in Bobby Kennedy's shoes; on the other they imagine what it was like to listen to him on that fateful day in Indianapolis.

Kennedy's eulogy of Martin Luther King Jr. was one of his best political speeches. His speech exemplified classical rhetorical training and demonstrated his command of language and memory. But his speech is memorable and moving because he identified with his audience—an audience in many ways starkly different from himself. Yet Kennedy spoke to what they shared: an experience of pain, deep sadness, and a longing for a better society. Students of public address appreciate the art and skill of this approach, and hopefully are inspired toward understanding and compassion.

Notes

1. John M. Murphy, "'A Time of Shame and Sorrow': Robert F. Kennedy and the American Jeremiad," *Quarterly Journal of Speech* 76 (1990): 401–14.

2. Karl W. Anatol and John R. Bittner, "Kennedy on King: The Rhetoric of Control," *Today's Speech* 16, no. 3 (September 1968): 31–34.

3. Kathleen Hall Jamieson, *Eloquence in an Electronic Age: The Transformation of Political Speechmaking* (New York: Oxford University Press, 1988).

Shouting at Your Neighbor
Why We Bother with Other Peoples' Languages

David I. Smith, Foreign Languages

Imagine yourself in a German class. As the class begins, you are looking at a black-and-white photo projected onto a large screen at the front of the room.[1] The instructor asks what you see. You say, three young people. Two are male, one female, and one of them is wearing a military uniform.

"No, look closer," the teacher says.

You realize that there is a fourth person partially hidden behind one of the folk in the foreground . . . wait, there's a fifth just visible on the right. You begin to slow down, letting the easy answers recede and really attending to the details. Stretching your limited German, you and the rest of the class work together to describe the people in the picture: their dress, their age, their expressions, their feelings.

They look grim—why? What might be happening? As more pictures are added, you find yourself exploring the story of some German students who set themselves to resist the Third Reich and ended up being beheaded by the authorities. The story has been made into a movie three times in Germany so far. (The next class, you will watch one of them.)

New questions bubble up: What motivated these young people? What role did their faith play? What would you have done in similar circumstances? Why has this story stayed alive in Germany across the intervening years? What role does it play in the stories that make up present-day German culture? You dig deeper, learning to read about, listen to, watch, and retell the story in German. This gives you plenty of chances to build your language skills, and those emerging skills enable you to fully hear this story as you gain access to interviews, film clips, and articles that are inaccessible to those who speak only English. As all of this unfolds, you begin to build new connections with people from outside your own circle of experience, people whose attempts to live faithfully in their cultural context might have something to say to you here and now.

Of course, this is one particular class, and other language classes will differ. But it is enough to give us a starting point for considering what language classes ought to look like and why we should bother with them. The structure of the class I've just described says, among other things, that the lives of others matter, that slowing down and learning to attend to them pays dividends, and that language skills are not just for our own immediate benefit. A language class can be one of the places where we learn to break out of life revolving around our own perspectives and ambitions. It can be a place where we learn to listen to those who are not like us, to love our neighbor who grew up in a different place, to show willingness to take a step in their direction to see what we might receive and what we might have to give.

Beyond Personal Contacts

Let's step back and explore those thoughts from a wider angle. People's personal reasons for studying a language vary quite widely. For some, career concerns are at the forefront—some of my recent German students (and of course wherever I mention German or, later, French, you can substitute other languages) have ended up doing things as varied as working for export companies, teaching in Switzerland, and helping curate museum exhibits about the Holocaust. For others, family history plays a key role, for many families contain speakers of more than one language. Some, for academic, professional, or personal reasons, need to read books and articles written elsewhere; I have students who need another language in order to be able to progress in their study of art history, theology, or musicology. For some, the exhilaration of combining new words in new ways and discovering fresh ways to think and speak is motivation enough.

Hovering behind all of these particular reasons is the simple reality that the people with whom we share the world (whichever language "we" think sounds like home) do not all communicate like us. In fact, that's too mild a way of putting it, as if most of the world speaks the way we do, with just a few tricky exceptions. Did you know that, by latest count, there are close to seven thousand languages in the world? And well over four billion people (a clear majority) who do not speak English? Over three hundred languages are spoken by people living in the United States. If you spend all your time with people who sound like you, you may not have to face this every day. But as travel increases and populations everywhere become more diverse, your chances of never running into speakers of other languages are decreasing. If you live in a town of any size and communicate only with English speakers, chances are that this is not because there are only English speakers around, but because your group of personal contacts is too limited. Language differences are all around us, and dealing with them well is an increasingly important skill.

The Failure of Red-Faced Shouting

Gaining language skills is not just for one's own benefit. Basic language skills can serve others' needs in very concrete ways—and it does not take advanced levels of fluency to make a difference. A few years ago I was at a large, international airport preparing to board a flight to Europe. The usual assorted collection of people was gathered at the gate, generally weary and a little too warm on a midsummer afternoon. As I moved toward the gate, I couldn't help but notice a difficult conversation taking place off to one side—"difficult" as in experiencing complete failure to communicate.

A burly security officer, uniformed and armed, had drawn a young woman from the line. She looked maybe twenty, dressed casually and carrying a small backpack. The officer, who towered over her, and whose visibly low level of patience betrayed a hard day already behind him, was asking questions about how much currency she was carrying and about what she had in her backpack. It was obvious that she barely understood a word he was saying. As I drew nearer I could hear her protesting as much, in German, with the odd word of broken English. "Ich verstehe nicht!" ("I don't understand!") His communication strategy, faced with someone who did not understand English, was to get louder and more insistent as she became more flustered and less able to figure out how to respond. A moment's thought will reveal that if someone does not understand something, saying it louder is unlikely to help, and yet when folk who are locked inside a single language find that not everyone's ears are attuned to the way they speak, it is not uncommon to find them reacting this way. It was not a happy exchange for either one of them, and it had reached gridlock. The stakes were high for both: she wanted to fly home, and he needed to know whether he should let her, but they were stuck.

I stepped over and offered to help, telling the officer that I could speak German and could translate for him if he wanted. With a combination of relief and poor grace, he agreed and told me his questions. The information needed was actually pretty simple, and the language needed to resolve the situation was at a level that a conscientious first- or second-year student could handle: What was in the bag? How much money did she have? It took only a few moments to explain the questions and relay the young woman's answers. Relief all around. A small disaster was kept from turning into a large one, a small moment of reconciliation was quietly celebrated, thanks were exchanged, and we each went on our way.

Just this past month I was relating this to one of my students, and he told me a very similar story. (They are not as rare as you might think.)

It reminds me of my last night during my semester in Grenoble. I was sitting in a hotel lobby where I had spent the night in order to catch a very early train to Grenoble the next morning. A beefy American man, already red faced, walked in and began to check in with the concierge. All the man wanted

137

was to ensure that he could receive calls from the outside of the hotel to his room. The two, neither well-versed in the other's language, completely miscommunicated, and yelling and frustration ensued. Finally the concierge turned to me. "Parlez vous anglais?" ("Do you speak English?") he asked, defeated. "Oui, je suis americain, en fait" ("Yes, in fact I am American"), I replied, and thirty seconds later the situation was resolved—and I had some very nice compliments on my French.

Here again, a modest amount of French was enough to cut through frustration and to help things run more smoothly. This student was able to act as a peacemaker. (Remember Jesus calling peacemakers blessed?)

Language learning is not just about us and our plans and ambitions. It's about how we share the world with people, and what kind of people we become as we live with language differences all around us.

The World and Your Mother

As we've seen, when people who cannot speak one another's language run up against one another, the results can be less than pretty: misunderstandings, resentments, exasperation, or just blank incomprehension and a missed opportunity to connect. But the problem is not merely the different words and grammar we use (which is why a language class that is only about words and grammar is not going to help as much as it could). The difficulties get compounded by the fact that our attachment to our own language and to the culture that is rolled up in it runs rather deep. We tend to experience our own language as apt and true, a way of speaking that matches reality and sends us signals that we are at home in the world and know how to navigate.

Our attachment to particular ways of speaking starts early. The ingenious use of baby pacifiers connected to computers has made it possible to research how newborns react to hearing different languages. Babies were given a choice between two recordings—suck faster to get one, or suck more slowly to get the other—and their choices were tracked. It was found that given a choice between hearing a story that their mothers had read aloud during the last month of the pregnancy and hearing a new story, newborns preferred the one they had heard before. They also preferred their mothers' languages over others. These preferences seem to begin to form when babies become able to hear sounds from outside the womb, during the final months of pregnancy. Of course, they are not understanding the words at this point (or for a while yet), but every language has its own rhythms, its own melodies. Try saying aloud "Once upon a time there were three little pigs." Now hum the sentence, not articulating the words, but keeping the same rising and falling patterns in your voice. That's the intonation pattern, the melody of your speech, and the first part of your native language that you heard as an infant. The rhythm and melody of your mother tongue began to sound comforting while you were still in the womb. Already by the time you are born, you prefer to have the world sound like your mother.

The process that started so early continues as you grow up. Children learn actual words from their parents and others around them, then sentences to organize those words, and then stories to tell. Words do not generally come to us from the dictionary but from people, carrying echoes of the ways that those around us have used them. Perhaps your mother always spoke of "blueberry pie" with a particular note of joy and longing, or of "soccer fans" with a faint hint of disdain, or of "liberal" politicians with implicit admiration or rejection. We learn the ways of going about life that count as normal in our context. Our parents do not usually tell us, for instance, that using a knife and fork rather than our fingers is polite in this cultural context but not in other places; they just make sure we understand it's polite. Our sense of comfort with particular ways of speaking, acting, and thinking grows as we do, though it also has to stretch and adjust as life gets more complex.

Language and culture are deeply woven together. For example, in one study of how parents interact with small children, Japanese and American parents were observed playing with their young children using a toy truck. An American mother would typically show the child the truck and point to its features—"See, it has wheels!" A Japanese mother would more often practice politeness—"You give the truck to me. Thank you!" An American cultural preference for doing things with objects around us and a Japanese cultural tendency to always think of oneself in relation to other people are reflected in these behaviors. Thus it is no surprise that the Japanese language contains a complex set of ways of expressing politeness to other people while speaking. Compared with Americans, German people typically keep a stronger distinction between their friends (people they know well and build friendships with over time) and their acquaintances (people they meet in public settings through the day). Accordingly, the German language has different ways of addressing people that reflect these different kinds of relationships. Communicating successfully with Germans involves not only getting these bits of grammar right but also being able to read these different relationship patterns so that you can rightly assess a situation and speak without giving offense. Language is about far more than grammar—one reason why machine translation only gets us so far, even when it works.

If we have to communicate in more than one language while very young, we adapt fairly easily—many children grow up speaking two or more languages. Probably well over half of the world's population is bilingual. If we are confronted with the challenge of communicating in another language later in life, then the task is more daunting. Our identity is in place, we have mastered familiar ways of speaking, and having to become like a child and start over with a new language can be humbling and hard work. The challenge is perhaps a little harder still if our first language is English. At various times in history, different languages have come to the forefront on the world stage. Languages such as Sanskrit, Aramaic, Arabic, Greek, Latin, French, Spanish, and Russian have at different times dominated substantial sections of the world as the cultures that spoke them achieved military or economic mastery. For the moment, English is the most dominant world language. It has always been harder to persuade the powerful to learn the languages of the less powerful. If my culture is powerful, it's easier to sit back and rely on others' efforts to learn my way of speaking.

Loving Foreigners

Looking at things through Christian eyes can give us some perspective. The pursuit of dominance and a preference for having others serve my needs are not New Testament recommendations. Jesus summarized the Law and the Prophets in two commandments: "'Love the Lord your God

141

with all your heart and with all your soul and with all your strength and with all your mind'; and, 'Love your neighbor as yourself'" (Luke 10:27). He was quoting both of these from the Old Testament. The second one, about loving one's neighbor, comes from the book of Leviticus, where it is soon followed by a command that echoes it but with a twist. "Love your neighbor as yourself," says Leviticus 19:18. Verse 34 continues: "The foreigner residing among you must be treated as your native-born. Love them as yourself, for you were foreigners in Egypt." In other words, treat foreigners the way you would want to be treated as a foreigner, love them as you love yourself. As Jesus put it on another occasion, "In everything, do to others what you would have them do to you" (Matthew 7:12). Don't go through life as if others are just there to serve you; they matter to God as surely as you do, and seeking their good is a way to imitate your Father in heaven. Being willing to learn another's language, to go through the effort and persistence needed to speak to others in ways that resonate with *their* hearts, being willing to listen to and learn from *their* stories, is one form that this commitment to being there for others can take.

Notice I said *one* form. Not all of us have equal opportunities or resources to engage in serious language learning. Some of us may still lead very linguistically sheltered lives. But if your educational path offers chances to learn a second (or a third) language, and to persist with it beyond survival level so that you can really get inside it, communicate with its speakers, and hear their stories, you should not pass up the opportunity. Grasp the chance to expand your linguistic capabilities. Resist the misconception that if language learning does not come quickly and easily to you then it is beyond you; it takes patient effort for the vast majority of us. Look for classes that do not reduce language to spelling and grammar; a quality foreign language course these days should include learning about culture and how to communicate effectively across cultural differences. Its focus should be not just words on worksheets, or learning to buy consumer goods at foreign stores and restaurants, or proving that you know a lot of terms for subtle sentence constructions. The riches and intricacies of language itself certainly have their place, but alongside them should come a process of beginning to enter into the experiences of those who speak and think in another tongue.

Connecting across Cultures

Seek out classes that make room for this kind of human connection across cultures (through movies, role plays, old photos of students who died for their convictions, or a wide range of other media). Don't let false comparisons daunt you—unless you are willing to assert that taking beginning science courses is a waste of time because you do not come out with Einstein's capabilities, or English is a waste of time because you can't write like Shakespeare. Let go of the idea that the measure of success is whether you are as fluent as a native speaker a few courses into your learning. Complete fluency takes time and effort to achieve, and need not be everyone's goal. But you can communicate meaningfully and make rich new connections far before you get there.

Hard work as it is (and I would not want to pretend otherwise), there are rich rewards to be found in the process of learning another language. New ways of thinking are opened up by new words and expressions that reflect a fresh way of looking at the world. Strange sounds and hilarious mistakes can add amusement if you are at all willing

143

to laugh at yourself. New realms of music, literature, and information are opened up by access to material that is not in English. New career skills and opportunities to serve can be created by the ability to work in more than one language. New connections and relationships become possible across cultural lines as you become able to hear what speakers of other languages have to say and share your own ideas with them.

These kinds of learning make us less likely to end up shouting at the world, unable to make headway unless we hear something like our own voice echoing back. Whether in airports, business meetings, workplaces, stores, restaurants, or on street corners, knowing more than one language can make you a reconciler. It creates opportunities to be a peacemaker, someone who can inject a little relief into the frictions and frustrations of cross-cultural communication. In the process, you will gain as much as you give if you are willing to open your horizons to the lives and stories of those who share this world but grew up in other languages and cultures. It's not just about you, but about how your life comes to relate to the life of your neighbor. Language can unite or divide us. A little learning can tip the balance.[2]

Notes

1. You can view this photograph at http://en.wikipedia.org/wiki/File:WhiteRose.jpg.

2. Various sources were used for the information in this chapter. You can read about the research on infants in *The Ascent of Babel: An Exploration of Language, Mind, and Understanding* by Gerry T. A. Altmann (Oxford: Oxford University Press, 1997) and find out more about cultural differences in upbringing in *The Geography of Thought: How Asians and Westerners Think Differently . . . and Why* by Richard Nisbett

(New York: The Free Press, 2004). The thoughts about cultural difference and a Christian response to it are explored at greater length in *Learning from the Stranger: Christian Faith and Cultural Diversity* by David I. Smith (Eerdmans, 2009). I would like to thank Jared Warren for sharing his experiences in France.

New Life from Ancient Texts

David Noe, Classics

Imagine a world in which nearly every rock, tree, and stream possesses a living, breathing power. This power has a face, in some cases two, and a name. It is personal and must be prayed to and placated with gifts and offerings of grain, flowers, or livestock if you want to prosper. If you want to guarantee that your newborn son enters the world safely, then you make your way to a grove of lotuses on the Esquiline Hill and pray to Juno Lucina. "O goddess," you might say, "who with Jupiter and Minerva directs the affairs of gods and men, see these fine sheaves of grain that I lay on your altar. Notice, mighty queen, the purity of my heart and the strength of my prayers. Grant, I humbly ask, that my son be born soon and his mother live through the labor, that he learn to speak and defend me against my enemies in the market and in court. I pray to you, Lucina, Hestia, Prorsa Postverta, and any other goddesses who might hear and attend my sacrifice." This is a world suffused and overflowing with divine power that wells from brook and forest glen.

Next picture an urban landscape along whose broad streets march manifold pillars. On the periphery of this sprawling city a breathtaking marvel towers; the trunks of its 127 columns stretch like marble trees 100 feet toward the sky. They support a broad and massive roof built of aromatic cedar beams. All along its length on the frieze are carved images of the gods at peace and war, beautiful images of creatures that look like men and women but are far larger and more magnificent; every bare muscle and shapely curve is formed and polished perfectly.

Through the bustling market near the temple's foot you can see a small, balding man speaking to a crowd of onlookers. He is proclaiming a God who does not live in a temple built by human hands and who has no need of sacrifices. The man says that though this God is greater in beauty and power than anyone can imagine, he must not be depicted in statues or portraits. Instead, this God has himself become human in the person of his son, a poor and humble peasant from the backwater province of Judea, and that same man was crucified as a criminal but rose again in the flesh three days later.

The crowd of onlookers from all over Asia Minor, speakers of Greek, Lydian, Latin, and so forth, looks at the strange speaker—whose name is Paul—with a mixture of curiosity and contempt.

This quick sketch gives some sense of the sharp contrast that early generations of pagans felt when they first compared the claims of the Christian gospel to their own well-developed and ancient faith. The early Greeks and Romans were avowedly and self-consciously religious. The spark of the divine, or *sensus divinitatis* as later generations called it, smoldered and smoked in their hearts, bursting forth in many bright displays of the finest art, literature, science, and architecture of the time. The magnificent temple of Artemis described above; the epic poems of Homer and Ovid; and the inventions and discoveries of thinkers like Archimedes, who worked out a formula for the volume of a cone, and Eratosthenes, who without sophisticated tools measured the earth's circumference—these were the fruits of their reverential care for the gods whom they feared and worshiped.

Nowhere is this reverential care more evident than in the Parthenon at Athens. The Athenians built this exquisite temple to honor the goddess who granted them victory over the advancing Persians. Even in its dilapidated state today, the temple is majestic. It is said that, like the human body, the Parthenon contains not one straight line. Instead, every step, pillar, beam, and cornice runs with some gentle slope or curve, cleverly fooling the eye and correcting for various optical flaws in the way we view the world. Most remarkable is that the statues adorning the temple's pediments were finished in the round. In other words, the back portions of these statues were as carefully sculpted as the fronts, though they would never be seen. Indeed, it was not until these statues were removed from the Parthenon by a British noble in the early 1800s, twenty-two hundred years after they were first set in place, that it was discovered that the statues were finished all round.

Why would the Athenians bother to perfect the parts of their statues that they thought no human eye would ever behold? What kind of a culture devotes such incredible time and care to what apparently is inconsequential? The answer lies in the ancient religious perspective: the temple of Athena was made for gods, not for mortals. Those hidden parts of the temple mattered because the gods could see them.

It has been rightly said that there was no true atheism in antiquity. While some groups, like the Epicurean philosophers, taught that the gods were distant and unconcerned with human affairs, too involved in elevated pleasures to care about us, no one would have dared to say that the gods did not exist. Instead, life was permeated at all levels with religious feeling, and the ancients found it impossible to escape the all-seeing eye of heaven.

The situation has changed since Socrates strolled the streets of Athens. These days the gods are not ritually consulted before war is made. Sacrifices are not offered before ambassadors are sent to foreign nations. Nonreligious, purely human interests are said to motivate the pursuits of science, literature, and art. Religion is thought to be optional. Claims of supernatural experience are dismissed. If our perspective is so different now, why study those ancient times? I will offer two reasons.

First, studying the classics teaches us compassion. The classics invite us to suffer with those who are at once both very much like us and yet also quite different. When the character Aeneas in Vergil's epic arrives on the shores of North Africa after being tossed by the wind, the majority of his fleet lost to a tempest sent by the angered Juno, he wanders into the rising city of Carthage. There, to his astonishment, he beholds paintings on the unfinished temples. These depict people whom he knew and who had fought in the war before Troy's lofty walls. He sees the great Achilles, kingly Priam, and the other heroes who struggled in the ten-year conflict. And then at last he sees himself also displayed, warring on the plain. As he chokes back his weeping, Aeneas comments to his squire that this land, Carthage, is truly civilized, for here "tears are shed for human suffering and mortal woes touch the heart."[1] The proof for Aeneas that he will receive a hospitable welcome in this new land is that he finds works of art that depict human suffering in a sympathetic way. People cry, they mourn for the hardship of others. With that confidence, Aeneas continues to the center of Carthage.

Today we might not think of simple weeping as a leading indicator of humanity and civilization. We might rather expect a well-developed culture to be marked by a working legal system or the pursuit of scientific knowledge. But for Vergil a city that knew how to express compassion was a healthy and hospitable city. We would do well to learn this lesson from the classical world. It is compassion that breaks down the barriers of skin color, language, and past conflict. It is compassion that prepares the way for peace and provides the basis of a true humanism.

The humanism of the Greeks and Romans recognized the innate connectedness of all people and diagnosed the state of the human condition as one of perpetual sorrow and brokenness. Both themes were developed in classical literature. For instance, the Roman playwright Terence once described the connectedness: "I am a human being, and thus I count nothing human as foreign to me."[2] And more than a century later the Roman poet Ovid, a great student of human nature, wrote, "I see and commend my better impulses, but the worse ones are what I follow."[3] These two facts of human existence—our connectedness through common experiences and our pitiful brokenness—are what make compassion both possible and necessary. This, then, is the first lesson to learn from the classics, the lesson of compassion.

The second reason for studying the ancient world is to prevent cultural memory loss. We should never forget that it is possible for a civilization to flourish under the assumption that the human world intersects with the divine. It is important to remember that religious sensibilities need not be aberrations. These days it is all too easy to become overly content, dangerously preoccupied, and proudly smug because of our modern achievements. Our vision can become shortsighted. The late Hugh Lloyd-Jones puts the matter succinctly like this:

> One of the best reasons for studying the past is to protect oneself against that insularity in time which restricts the uneducated and those who write to please them. The ordinary man feels superior to the men of past ages, whose technology was inferior to what he is used to and whose ethical and political beliefs were not those which he has been taught to consider as the only right ones.[4]

Our insularity in time can close us off to supernatural possibilities. Today's world encourages us to purge from our minds any backward notions of divine intervention and providence. But it would be a mistake to think we have transcended the moral and spiritual limitations that our forebears felt so keenly. Our modern knowledge is powerful, but it is not *that* powerful.

I have offered two important reasons for reading classical literature: developing compassion and avoiding cynicism in matters divine. There are other benefits, of course, like being able to think more clearly, write more expressively, and appreciate more deeply 2,000 years of art, architecture, and poetry that are built upon the classics. This sort of education enrolls you in a republic of letters, where you can talk and argue with some of the world's brightest (and most anguished) souls, men and women like Sappho, Plato, Marcus Aurelius, and St. Ambrose.

But where does the Apostle Paul fit in that conversation? As you will recall, we left him standing at the base of the great temple of Artemis in Ephesus, preaching to a hostile crowd. That angry mob laid hold of Paul's companions Gaius and Aristarchus and rushed toward the theater. There, for more than two hours, in an amazing display of true religious fervor, they chanted, "Great is Artemis of the Ephesians!" (Acts 19:29–34).

The chanting pagans were quite surprised by the claims made by Christ's followers. The reason for this, however, was not what you might expect. They did not think it unusual that a god would walk among men. When Paul and Barnabas, for example, came through the region of Lystra, their wonder-working and teaching so astonished the locals that they designated Paul Hermes and Barnabas Zeus. Nor did they think it strange that blood must be shed for the remission of sins. All their rituals included sacrifice of some sort. What surprised them most about the Christian gospel was the message of divine humility and of a bodily resurrection. The message that Paul and others brought was foolishness to the Greeks: God took on human form and walked among us, died, and rose again. He had not come down among mortals to sleep around or punish his enemies, but to fulfill the law and pray for those who persecuted him. Immortality had clothed itself with mortality, and the proof of his divine Godhead was that his body did not see decay.

The deeply religious people of the ancient world were stunned by this unexpected display of power in humility. Their philosophers and poets had carefully cultivated a true humanism for many centuries before Christ's incarnation. Each one took the inheritance he had received and worked to improve upon it, developing and ornamenting the basic themes of courage, moderation, wisdom, and justice. But while authors like Sophocles and Aristophanes knew something was rotten at the core of human nature, they were unable to imagine a God who becomes human in order to purify what is rotten and who is brutalized by his enemies for love of his people. There are no true parallels to the incarnation or resurrection in classical literature. The God-man changed things forever.

Nevertheless, Paul knew his audiences shared his belief that all men and women are inherently religious. For their part, Christians have held onto this belief, sometimes stating it this way: each of us has an impulse to praise and glorify our Creator. Expressions of this idea can be found in some of the Reformation's foundational documents, like the *Belgic Confession*, which states that we all know God because the "universe is before our eyes like a beautiful book in which all creatures, great and small, are as letters to make us ponder the invisible things of God." Such are the Christian echoes of Paul's assertion that we know God "from what has been made" (Romans 1:20).

But as we noted previously, times have changed. In our age there are many who say they have no sense of the divine and no understanding of religious talk. To connect with such people Christians will have to redouble their efforts to speak to the human condition, the nature of suffering, and the inescapable need for comfort. Perhaps through such efforts they will begin to pry open the modern religious imagination, so that a new but ancient light can shine in. This aspiration was expressed in the twentieth century with these words:

How would it be if human nature could be founded upon some secure rock, in order that then the architect might start to build once more, and build, this time, with a conscience void of offense? Such is the Christian ideal, the ideal of a loftier humanism—a humanism as rich and as joyful as the humanism of Greece, but a humanism founded upon the grace of God.[5]

Notes

1. Vergil, *The Aeneid*, I.462. All translations are my own.

2. Terence, *The Self-Punisher*, line 77.

3. Ovid, *The Metamorphoses*, book 7, line 20.

4. Hugh Lloyd-Jones, *The Justice of Zeus*, 2nd ed. (Berkeley, CA: University of California Press, 1983), 156.

5. J. Gresham Machen, *The Origin of Paul's Religion* (New York: Macmillan, 1921), 224.

An Invitation

Won Lee, Biblical Studies

It came in a tattered yellow envelope that had obviously taken a long journey through the mail. It was an invitation to speak on Judaism at the School of Foreign Languages at Peking University, the most prestigious university in China. I was excited, puzzled, and worried as I read. What an opportunity for me to teach the Old Testament to rising young intellectuals in China! Imagine the potential impact on their thinking about Judaism and Christianity. But why was such an invitation issued by a language school, instead of a religion or philosophy department? Was there a hidden agenda that might cause trouble for my ongoing involvement in spreading the gospel in China?

In any case, the letter spelled out clearly what would be expected from me: I could choose any topic, as long as it was related to Judaism. But I must not attempt to proselytize students, I should not approach the issue apologetically, and I would be strictly prohibited from sharing my personal testimony. No doubt the school wanted me to treat Judaism as a purely academic subject and address its significance in a completely objective manner.

I found myself in a moral and intellectual dilemma as I considered the invitation. I am an Old Testament scholar but not an expert on Judaism per se. Even if I were, I'm not sure that it would be possible for me to teach the Hebrew Bible, the normative sacred scripture for Judaism and Christianity, as merely an ancient artifact. I am a Christian, whose heart and mind have been comforted, disturbed, and excited by the living Word of God. I try to listen to it carefully, chew on it rigorously, teach it responsibly, and live it out as best I can in every waking moment. Acknowledging this tension, but not wanting to miss the opportunity, I accepted the invitation, wondering whether I could leave my faith at the door in my lecture.

Then came what seemed like months of preparation. I chose a topic that has been important in most cultures through all of history: the social roles of men and women. This issue is tied to Judaism by the fact that the Hebrew Bible was widely accepted—in the West at least—as an authoritative source of God-given laws and social norms. I decided to focus my lecture on the first three chapters of Genesis, where we read about the creation of a man and a woman and about their fall away from God. These chapters have been interpreted in various ways to answer the question, should men have status and authority over women? I hoped that by examining various answers to this question I could convince my audience that studying the Bible is important for understanding societies that have been shaped by Jewish or Christian influences.

When I finally made it to Peking University in China, I found myself in front of 180 students in a large auditorium. I now invite you to hear what they heard, to read the biblical text along with me, to hear what the text says, and to think about how we interpret that text. For this is the kind of wrestling and grappling with issues that students of Bible and theology participate in during their classes. Come and listen.

In the biblical account, God's creation of Man takes place before God's creation of Woman (Genesis 2:7, 22). This ordering of events has led many to believe that Man's authority over Woman is divinely ordained. In the ancient Near East it was traditional to acknowledge the most important person, or the person with the highest social status, before acknowledging anyone else. And so when God's Word gives Man chronological priority, it appears to grant him status and authority over Woman. Even the New Testament seems to affirm the importance of this idea: "A woman should learn in quietness and full submission. I do not permit a woman to teach or to assume authority over a man; she must be quiet. For Adam was formed first, then Eve" (1 Timothy 2:11–13).

Some readers say Genesis 2 provides additional evidence that God created Woman with an inferior status. They point out two details beyond the chronology. First, referring to the description of God creating Woman from one of Man's ribs, some suggest that she has a secondary or "derivative" status—that she depends on Man for her existence. Second, some claim that according to the text, Woman was created only to be Man's "helper," and so her ordained place is under his authority.

Then there are those who claim Woman is inferior because she is the one who fell prey to temptation in the Garden of Eden. They find support for this view in 1 Timothy 2:14, which says (continuing the passage quoted above), "And Adam was not the one deceived; it was the woman

159

who was deceived and became a sinner." The suggestion seems to be that Woman alone was responsible for breaking God's prohibition, "But you must not eat from the tree of the knowledge of good and evil, for when you eat of it you will certainly die" (Genesis 2:17). It was her disobedience that led to the couple's expulsion from the Garden of Eden. If only the Woman had resisted the temptation of the serpent! No more hard work, labor pains, fighting against nature. Were it not for her, humans could live with the Creator in the Garden of Eden happily ever after!

But of course there are those who believe these interpretations to be distortions of God's holy Word, and many have offered alternative interpretations.

Some have argued that Genesis does not actually say Man was created before Woman. It says only that God formed "Adam" (*adam* in Hebrew) of dust from the ground (*adamah* in Hebrew), making the first human literally an earthly being, neither male nor female. From this being God made Woman and, while doing so, differentiated the sexes. According to this interpretation, Adam became male only when his female counterpart was created. Who, then, was specifically created first, Man or Woman?

Others have suggested that the creation of Woman from Man's rib implies nothing about her inferiority. Wasn't Adam made out of dirt from the ground? Is dirt more valuable than a rib? What was Adam's own contribution in making a woman? Did he know God's plan to make Woman out of him? Wasn't he unconscious? Doesn't the story imply that the Woman is made of the same stuff as the Man, and doesn't this fact suggest that she is his equal? In any case, isn't the main focus of the narrative on *who* made Woman, rather than *from what* she was made?

Furthermore, many deny that there are negative connotations in the statement that Woman was "a helper suitable for him [i.e., Adam]" (Genesis 2:18). Does being a helper indicate a lower status? In Psalm 54:4 God himself is called our helper. Surely the very reason God created Woman was because Man's state of being alone was not "good." How could it be possible for Man to fulfill God's blessings to humanity—"be fruitful and increase in number" (Genesis 1:28)—without Woman?

Finally, when it comes to interpreting the story in Genesis 3:1–6, many believers are reluctant to pin more guilt on Eve than on Adam. What if Adam was there all along while Eve was tempted by the serpent? The biblical account is open to this interpretation, for whenever the serpent and the Woman address each other, they use "we" and the plural form of "you," as if Adam is a silent observer. And there is no time lapse between the Woman's eating and her giving the forbidden fruit to the Man: "She also gave some to her husband, who was *with* her" (Genesis 3:6, emphasis added). Wasn't the Man primarily at fault for eating the fruit, since the prohibition had been given to him alone prior to creation of the Woman? Why else would God punish Adam, if he were not accountable for his own actions?

Having outlined so many different interpretations, I stopped to let my audience think about this general observation: It is not so simple to interpret this passage of Genesis, is it? It is difficult for readers to know for sure that their interpretation is the right one. This is why conversations about the Bible continue even today. I wanted the Chinese students to understand that people committed to the authority of Scripture have debated these issues for centuries. We shouldn't be surprised to find echoes of these debates when we study societies that have historical connections to Judeo-Christian traditions.

To illustrate this point I concluded my lecture by showing images of historic works of art that raise questions about the interpretation of Genesis 3. Only someone familiar with the text would be able to look at these works and discern the relevant questions:

- A catacomb fresco of Adam and Eve (third century), acknowledging the presence of Adam as Eve touched the tree. *Did Adam actively participate in taking the forbidden fruit?*

- Gislebertus's *Temptation of Eve* (1120), presenting Eve gazing forward with her right arm supporting her head while the left hand sneaks backward to grasp an apple. *Was Eve searching for anyone who might see her taking the fruit?*

- Hugo van der Goes's *Original Sin* (1468), portraying the serpent as part man and part lizard staring at Eve, who is about to take fruit from the tree (meanwhile, Adam extends his left hand ready to receive the fruit). *Does the unsure facial expression of Adam represent his guilt? Does the confident look of Eve suggest her innocence, even as she reaches for yet another fruit?*

- Albrecht Dürer's *Adam and Eve* (1504), showing Eve taking the fruit from the mouth of the serpent, while Adam looks resolutely into Eve's eye. *Is Adam showing concern about the fate of Eve as he holds on to the branch of the Tree of Life?*

- Michelangelo's *Fall of Man and Expulsion from the Paradise* (1508–12), depicting the serpent as half woman and half snake, suggesting that Adam is fooled by the cunning beauty of the serpent woman. *Does Eve play no role in tempting Adam as he bypasses her to reach for the fruit?*

- Titian's *Fall of Man* (1570), showing the serpent as an innocent child and Eve gleefully taking the fruit as Adam touches her breast. *Did Adam try to stop Eve's defiant act?*

- Rembrandt's *Adam and Eve* (1638), showing the dragon-like serpent stretching ominously above Adam and Eve, who seem confused and bewildered as they argue about whether to take the fruit. *Did Adam try to persuade Eve not to eat the fruit?*

This final exercise, though clearly inadequate due to my limited knowledge of art history, was meant to demonstrate that the Old Testament story is not dead or irrelevant. Rather, ancient texts have become classic precisely because of their enduring significance. Seeing how a biblical text was received and interpreted in later cultural contexts raises questions about the legitimacy of our own contemporary interpretations. The text becomes more than a "written" document; it becomes a "living" thing that demands a conscious conversation with contemporary readers. And as we bring our contemporary eyes to this story and its meanings, we wrestle with the very narratives that define our own ways of understanding the world. When we ask how Adam and Eve should have acted, we are asking deep questions about our own understanding of gender roles.

After the lecture there was a flood of questions, two of which still ring in my mind. First, *Did the rest of the Hebrew Bible place women in subordinate positions to their fathers and/or husbands?* Certainly in the text, I said, women are cursed to be ruled by their husbands (Genesis 3:16); women are easily dispensed to a hostile mob as a trade for the safety of house guests (Genesis 19:8); women are part of the property of the house (Exodus 20:17); and women are considered ritually unclean during their menstrual periods (Leviticus 12:2).

But to pursue this important question in more depth, I appealed to an old principle commonly used by Reformed Christians: each part of the Bible carries its own unique perspective but must be understood in light of the rest of Scripture. Genesis 1–3 contains just a few threads that are part of a great tapestry. Looking at those threads individually is like looking at the loose ends on the back of the tapestry. Only if we look at the front side will we see the overarching pattern, the creative art, and the recognizable intention. Likewise, the Bible in its entirety proposes an ideal of equality and unity between men and women—or, it is more correct to say, it presents a trajectory for how to reach such a harmonious union. Those who subscribe to the authority of the Bible are called to work toward this well-being (or shalom) and reconciliation: "There is neither Jew nor Gentile, neither slave nor free, nor is there male and female, for you are all one in Christ Jesus" (Galatians 3:28).

Careful reading of the Bible requires that one face diverse opinions on a single topic, view a text rooted in a particular historical and cultural context, read it in relation to others within the entire Bible, and formulate an overarching interpretive framework from which each opinion is valued and transformed. This principle appreciates the diversity in the Bible as a reflection of ongoing dialogue among its ancient writers and modern readers; it also warns us not to take one small set of texts to represent the entire biblical position. You will see such colorful contours of the biblical landscape when you take time to read it as a whole.

Now for the second question that the Chinese students raised: *Why should nonreligious people read the Bible seriously?* I was not prepared for this question, especially because I had been expected to leave my faith at the door. How would you respond? Is it enough to say that the Bible has played a foundational role in the birth and development of Western intellectual life throughout ages? It is true that in the multifaceted dimensions of Western civilization, including science, literature, law, and art, the presence of the Bible or the biblical tradition is undeniable. You could cite the influence of the Bible on authors such as Augustine, whose works profoundly changed human learning in the West, or books like the King James Bible, which fundamentally influenced how we use the English language. Even the liberal arts educational system cannot be fully understood apart from the scriptural inquiry of monasteries and other Christian communities in medieval Europe. For any educated individual, a solid biblical knowledge is required. Or, one familiar with Chinese culture might use a cherished Chinese proverb diplomatically: "Once you know yourself and your enemies, you will win any battle against them." Studying the Bible, then, may offer practical benefits for anyone interested in competing on a world stage or aspiring to a global citizenship.

But in addition, I suggested, the Bible offers helpful spiritual insights. The world of the Bible—manifested in its languages, cultural practices, and historical gaps—is intrinsically foreign to ours. To understand the meanings of the Bible through its foreignness invites all, including nonreligious people, to a conversation that—if it takes the claims of the ancient text seriously—must lead to spiritual reflection.

The obvious and yet more profound question came later. The student who asked it approached me after my lecture and spoke to me in a whispering voice. (I sensed that she was a member of a house church.) Why does the Bible *really* matter? she asked. How should a committed follower of Christ read the Word?

Because I had tried to leave my faith at the door in my lecture, I had failed to answer that deep question. In retrospect, I had failed to present what Genesis 1–3 really is: a sacred text. The Bible is more than an anthology or a textual repository for the ancient Hebrew and early Christian religious traditions; it is sacred and thus possesses authority. It embodies truth, or at least a truer understanding than other writings, about the way things should be. About good literature, we hold opinions; about sacred texts, we hold convictions. The sacredness of the Bible has been acknowledged and authenticated by the communities that regard it as Scripture. At the same time, the Bible has shaped the thought and life of these communities, who willingly submit to its authority. This dialogical relationship between the sacred text and the believing community forms the basis for each believer's interpretation of biblical texts, not merely as a collection of ancient religious writings but as authoritative, sacred, and *inspired*. The Bible possesses its own intrinsic message and value, for it is the Word of God. Yet, in order to give the Bible its due as sacred Scripture, one has to enter into the long history of interpretation in which what it says has interacted with how it is understood.

In many universities the modern discipline of biblical study demands that the Bible be only an object of critical analysis, not a subject of faith. Unconsciously, we have accepted such an assumption and adopted scientific attitudes in studying Scripture. Though we are doing so many good things (critically engaging with the text, advancing written and oral skills, appreciating diverse cultural and historical interpretations, utilizing creative pedagogical methods, prompting curiosity and imagination), we are doing them in a way that lets the "wisdom of this age" squeeze us into its own mold, blending into an educational ethos that desperately needs to be reformed. The Apostle Paul warns, "Do not conform to the pattern of this world, but be transformed by the renewing of your mind. Then you will be able to test and approve what God's will is—his good, pleasing and perfect will" (Romans 12:2). In other words, we cannot study Scripture fully and leave our faith at the door. Such study will always be inadequate.

The Bible is not a jewelry box, containing a variety of moral sayings that we can pick and choose to support our positions in a market of equal ideas.

Regrettably, I was put off guard by the student who approached me with her question, and my response to her was not very clear or eloquent. But this is what I should have said: read the Bible as Scripture; be open to being converted continually while conversing with it; taste its higher wisdom; be ready to plunge into God's revolution in a broken world. The Bible itself calls for such wisdom. Its voice does not promote and sanction the existing order; rather, it promotes a radical change in reality by emphasizing the conflict between God's will and human ambitions, between the kingdom of God and the dominion of the world. To do justice to the very nature of the Bible as sacred Scripture, we dare to accept the call of renewing our minds by incorporating faith into all of our rigorous scholarly analysis.

I had one other experience of teaching the Bible in China, this time to Chinese house church leaders. I can still see their suspicious and bewildered eyes staring at me. I came from the United States and spoke little Chinese. I raised my voice loudly and even more loudly as my hands moved up and down in my presentations. I am not completely sure what they heard from me, but during that visit, as we took seriously the claims of Scripture *to be Scripture*, I am certain that it was I who learned from them how to love God's Word. Their profound respect for the authority of the Word, their bottomless hunger for learning it, and their unpretentious piety shook me to the very core of my Christian identity.

I revisit that memory as I become more habitual in studying the Bible. The memory of the experiences with the house church leaders lifts my spirit. And that is what biblical studies, in the end, should do as well.

Notes

- Catacomb Fresco: http://jewishchristianlit.com/Topics/AdamNeve/a_n_e07.html

- Gislebertus's *Temptation of Eve*: http://www.sacred-destinations.com/france/autun-musee-rolin-photos/slides/xti_2801p

- Hugo van der Goes's *Original Sin*: http://jewishchristianlit.com/Topics/AdamNeve/a_n_e08.html

- Albrecht Dürer's *Adam and Eve*: http://www.metmuseum.org/toah/works-of-art/19.73.1

- Michelangelo's *Fall of Man and Expulsion from the Paradise*: http://jewishchristianlit.com/Topics/AdamNeve/michel06.html

- Titian's *Fall of Man*: http://jewishchristianlit.com/Topics/AdamNeve/a_n_e06.html
- Rembrandt's *Adam and Eve*: http://www.rembrandtpainting.net/rmbrdnt_selected_etchings/adam_and_eve.htm

Acknowledgments

This book testifies to the importance of education in the humanities. While each chapter gives a glimpse into a particular topical area, it also contributes to a widespread discussion about how people perpetuate values from generation to generation through texts, works of art, and educational systems. Each author benefited from just this kind of discussion during the writing process. In fact, even before they wrote their chapters, the authors met together to discuss various books and articles, and they made a plan for reaching college-bound students who are trying to find their vocational bearings. Those conversations involved other key individuals who deserve acknowledgment. First, the authors thank Shirley Roels for securing financial support through the Lilly Vocation Project at Calvin College. Additional funds, editorial advice, and proofreading and typesetting services came from the Office of the Provost of Calvin College and the Kuyers Institute for Christian Teaching and Learning. We are also extremely grateful to Jim Bratt for organizing and facilitating several of our group discussions. Our gratitude as well goes to Jacob Schepers, who so diligently tracked down websites that show artwork mentioned in some of the essays. Finally, it was immensely helpful to get feedback on our first draft from a high school focus group, and so we thank Nicholas DeKoster, Jenifer Gunnink, Claire Lambert, and Brendan Stafford for their careful reading and insightful comments.